Contents

Contents

INSTITUTE OF LEADERSHIP & MANAGEMENT ilm

SUPERSERIES

Ł. ıt

FOURTн

Published for the
Institute of Leadership & Management by

Pergamon
Flexible
Learning

OXFORD AMSTERDAM BOSTON LONDON NEW YORK PARIS
SAN DIEGO SAN FRANCISCO SINGAPORE SYDNEY TOKYO

Pergamon Flexible Learning
An imprint of Elsevier Science
Linacre House, Jordan Hill, Oxford OX2 8DP
200 Wheeler Road, Burlington, MA 01803

First published 1986
Second edition 1991
Third edition 1997
Fourth edition 2003

British Library Cataloguing in Publication Data
A catalogue record for this book is available from the British Library

ISBN 0 7506 5853 3

For information on Pergamon Flexible Learning
visit our website at www.bh.com/pergamonfl

Institute of Leadership & Management
registered office
1 Giltspur Street
London
EC1A 9DD
Telephone 020 7294 3053
www.i-l-m.com
ILM is a subsidiary of the City & Guilds Group

The views expressed in this work are those of the authors and do
not necessarily reflect those of the Institute of Leadership &
Management or of the publisher

Authors: Angus Thomas, Colin Everson and Dela Jenkins
Editor: Dela Jenkins
Editorial management: Genesys, www.genesys-consultants.com
Based on previous material by: Joe Johnson
Composition by Genesis Typesetting, Rochester, Kent
Printed and bound in Great Britain by MPG Books, Bodmin

Workbook introduction

1 ILM Super Series study links

This workbook addresses the issues of *Managing Lawfully – People and Employment*. Should you wish to extend your study to other Super Series workbooks covering related or different subject areas, you will find a comprehensive list at the back of this book.

2 Links to ILM qualifications

This workbook relates to the following learning outcomes in segments from the ILM Level 3 Introductory Certificate in First Line Management and the Level 3 Certificate in First Line Management.

C8.7   Maintaining Discipline
1 Understand the organization's employment policies and procedures, and the need to follow them implicitly
2 Maintain adequate records to support and enable the disciplinary process
3 Monitor individuals' compliance with organizational policies
4 Identify areas of concern
5 Recognize different attitudes and behaviours and their impact on the team
6 Support individuals to meet performance.

C8.8 Resolving Conflict
1 Recognize a range of conflict situations
2 Understand the ways in which conflict may develop and can be resolved
3 Evaluate the effects of conflict on performance and the individual
4 Observe and react to a variety of situations to minimize and resolve conflict
5 Work towards the creation of a positive and harmonious work environment.

3 Links to S/NVQs in Management

This workbook relates to the following element of the Management Standards which is used in S/NVQs in Management, as well as a range of other S/NVQs.

C15.2 Contribute to implementing disciplinary and grievance procedures.

It will also help you to develop the following personal competences:

- acting assertively
- behaving ethically.

4 Workbook objectives

Work is a vital part of life for the majority of people and occupies a large proportion of their adult lives. It is essential that people are managed fairly and that the policies and procedures that order their working lives are applied consistently for both individuals and identifiable groups of employees.

First line managers are the main interface for most employees between themselves and their employer's policies and procedures. First line managers have a significant influence on achieving harmonious relationships in every workplace.

For most people, most of the time, no major problems arise, and the formal aspects of management procedures are not the subject of debate. As a first line manager you can contribute to this favourable climate by knowing and implementing your organization's procedures implicitly.

You also need to have an appreciation of the underlying laws that have been developed over many years to provide the minimum standards that every employee, in any working situation, can expect to be applied. The law increasingly influences the way in which employers must frame their policies.

Trades unions came into being in an era when many employers exercised absolute powers over their staff and frequently abused those powers. The unions helped to establish reasonable minimum working conditions for employees. The unions' role has changed over the years, but they still represent the interests of millions of employees in a wide variety of occupations. Dealings with them are an everyday aspect of some first line managers' working lives.

In this workbook, we will look at some aspects of the management policies, procedures and approaches that help to create good working relationships. These are effective for 95% of the time with 95% of employees – and even more in well run organizations.

However, for those employers and employees who cannot, or will not, work within such policies, the law provides a framework that both parties must work within. First line managers need to be aware of that framework and use their skills, training and experience to ensure that the procedures are applied fairly and consistently.

4.1 Objectives

When you have worked through this workbook you will be better equipped to:

- comprehend and implement your organization's employment policies and procedures as a major step towards managing your team fairly and consistently within the law;
- manage your team to achieve positive relationships both with you and within the team, recognizing and defusing conflict in the first instance wherever practicable;
- deal with disciplinary matters in a fair and consistent way within the law.

5 Activity planner

The following activities require some planning, so you may want to look at these now.

- Activity 1 asks you to obtain a copy of your organization's employee or organization handbook.
- In Activity 20 you are asked to explain:
  - how well you ensure that your team members are kept informed of the organization's disciplinary procedures;
  - the actions you intend to take to make them better informed;
  - how confident you are that the contributions you make to implementing disciplinary and grievance procedures are consistent with your organization's values and policies;
  - if you are less than totally confident about the quality of your contributions, what actions you will take to improve them.
- Activity 29 asks some searching questions about whether you and your colleagues are consistent in treating individuals with respect, and in keeping disciplinary matters confidential.
- In Activity 37 a number of questions are asked regarding your disciplinary records.

Some or all of these Activities may provide the basis of evidence for your S/NVQ portfolio. All portfolio Activities and the Work-based assignment are signposted with this icon.

The icon states the elements to which the portfolio activities and Work-based assignment relate.

Session A
Employment policies

1 Introduction

All organizations must manage their affairs in every respect within the law of the land. In the employment field, there are many statute laws which apply, dealing with matters such as:

- contracts of employment;
- terms and conditions of employment;
- equal opportunities;
- data protection;
- dealings with trades unions;
- health, safety and welfare at work.

Full coverage of health and safety law is given in *Managing Lawfully – Health, Safety and Environment* in this series

The best way for an organization to ensure that it manages within the law is for it to develop employment policies that accord with both the letter and the spirit of existing laws and changes that are known to be forthcoming.

Provided that they do so, and provided that they revise their policies from time to time as the law and regulations change, managers (including you) can be confident that they are managing lawfully by implementing the policies implicitly.

In this session, we'll examine the policies that organizations need to implement, and the records that they need to keep in order to manage within the law.

2 Communicating employment policies

Whether or not an organization writes down its employment policies, it must obey the law consistently and fairly throughout its operations. An important aspect of doing so is communicating those policies to all its employees.

Three effective ways of doing this are through:

- providing an Employee Handbook;
- induction training;
- giving regular briefings to communicate changes in policy.

2.1 The organisation handbook

Activity 1 · 3 mins

Many references will be made to Employee Handbooks or manuals in this session. Please obtain a copy of your own organization's document to compare this text with. If your organization doesn't have one, then talk to your manager about possible actions once you have completed the session.

Many organizations communicate their employment policies by recording them in a handbook, which is issued to all employees when they first join. This is a crucial aspect of ensuring that everyone gets the same message.

But it isn't sufficient simply to issue an Employee Handbook. That is not considered to be communicating with employees adequately within the law.

Activity 2

3 mins

List three or more factors which may prevent employees from understanding the Employee Handbook issued to them on joining. For example, literacy – not every employee may be able to read, but everyone still needs to understand the organization's policies.

_____

_____

_____

The factors you may have listed include:

- language – some employees may not have English as their first language;
- organizational jargon that is unfamiliar to a newcomer;
- references to the organizational structure and specialist departments, which they are unfamiliar with;
- legalistic phrases such as 'gross misconduct', which may be new to them.

You may well have listed others, thinking back to your own early days with a new employer.

The handbook's content will vary according to the size of the organization and the facilities it is able to provide. But some items should appear in every handbook, especially those concerning health and safety, disciplinary procedures and grievance procedures.

Activity 3

5 mins

What employment procedures do you believe should be covered in an Employee Handbook? Make at least five suggestions.

_____

_____

_____

_____

_____

You may have suggested the following topics: hours of work; reporting absence for sickness or some other reason; holiday entitlement and booking procedure; maternity leave; pension schemes; health and safety; smoking; emergencies; personal hygiene; sports and social facilities; payment procedures; recognized trades unions; disciplinary and grievance procedures; definition of 'gross misconduct'; training and opportunities for development.

A sensible time to issue the Employee Handbook is immediately after induction has taken place.

2.2 Induction training

The importance of induction training as the first step in communicating employment policies cannot be overstated.

Ideally, induction should be delivered before employees begin work, otherwise they may be put at risk through ignorance of safety and emergency procedures. Also, it will be open to individuals to claim that 'nobody told me I wasn't supposed to do that', no matter how obviously wrong their conduct may seem to you.

Though 'ignorance of the *law* is no defence', many employment rules go beyond what the law requires, so ignorance of rules about use of property for personal purposes, or how to report absence, would only put an employee in breach of rules if they had been given reasonable instruction in them.

At induction, the main aspects of the organization's employment policies should be explained by competent managers. The new employees should be given a chance to ask questions and clarify anything which they do not understand. This may be especially important with young employees new to the world of work: they may find it a more disciplined environment than they have been used to.

2.3 Regular briefings

Holding regular meetings with your whole team has many advantages. It encourages team spirit, it makes everyone feel involved, no-one has an excuse that they haven't been informed of rules and regulations, and it enables you to obtain feedback about how the team members feel about the organization and the organizational policies that affect them.

3 The contract of employment

EXTENSION I and 2
You can get useful information on contracts of employment from the Advisory, Conciliation and Arbitration Service (ACAS).

The contract of employment is a legal document which sets out the agreement between an employer and an employee. In it, the employee agrees to do specified work in return for which the employer provides the necessary facilities to do the job and pays agreed remuneration.

3.1 Written terms and conditions of employment

It is a legal right for all employees working for organizations employing 20 staff or more to be issued with a written statement of terms and conditions of employment. This statement will specify in detail, for the individual employee, the topics covered generally in the Employee Handbook. It should include grievance and disciplinary procedures.

3.2 How can the contract be ended?

The contract can be broken by either party, for example:

■ If *employees* fail to return from holiday, and announce that they intend to remain abroad for the next five years, that would effectively break the contract. So would doing work for a competing company, or committing one of the offences defined as 'gross misconduct', such as fighting or deliberately damaging property.
■ If the *employer* fails to pay wages as agreed, or requires an employee to do work which training has not been provided for, or which is unsafe or illegal, then the employer will have broken the contract.

The simplest way for the contract to be ended is for the employee to resign, giving the notice required under the contract.

3.3 What remedies are available for breaches of contract?

If an employee breaks the contract, the remedies available to the *employer* will depend on the disciplinary procedures agreed. If the breach is sufficiently serious, dismissal is always available as the final sanction.

For the *employee*, there may be a remedy through the agreed grievance procedure. If the employee has been dismissed, or has resigned because they believe it is impossible to continue working for the employer, they can apply to an Employment Tribunal (formerly known as an Industrial Tribunal) for a remedy for unfair dismissal. The Tribunal may make an award in the employee's favour if they can convince its members that their case is a just one.

4 Employment Tribunals

Employment Tribunals are legal bodies appointed to adjudicate on legal disputes involving unfair dismissal, victimization, and discrimination on grounds of race, sex or disability. They consist of a 'chair', who is legally qualified, sitting with two other people: one with commercial experience and the other with a practical trade union background.

5 Grievance and disciplinary procedures

This session gives you a brief introduction to formal grievance and disciplinary procedures. You will learn more about them, and about the informal steps you can take in a disciplinary situation, in the rest of this workbook.

5.1 Formal grievance procedures

Formal grievance procedures are an important part of good practice within an organization's employment policies. They offer employees who feel that they are being unfairly treated the chance to raise the matter with their own management.

A credible grievance procedure has a number of stages, allowing the employee to raise their concern:

- initially with their immediate supervisor, team leader or manager;
- if that does not resolve the problem, then with the next manager in the hierarchy;
- and ultimately with a designated senior manager, possibly in the Personnel or Human Resources department.

Informal grievance procedures are a very important aspect of positive employment relations and, as such, will be dealt with more fully in Session B. Fairly implemented, they can prevent minor issues from growing into major ones that may become subject to the formal disciplinary procedure.

5.2 Formal disciplinary procedures

A common misconception is that discipline is about 'punishing' an individual for doing wrong. In fact, the aim of an effective disciplinary procedure is to help employees return to acceptable standards in whatever area necessary.

EXTENSION 3
ACAS is an independent body that can conciliate in employment matters. It produces a number of booklets to help managers work effectively within the law.

The Advisory, Conciliation and Arbitration Service (ACAS) publishes a Code of Practice on disciplinary procedures. Employers who follow this Code, both to the letter and in spirit, are likely to achieve more harmonious relationships with their employees and be able to show that they are managing within the law.

It is vital that you understand your organization's grievance and disciplinary procedures, as they may well affect you directly in your day-to-day activities.

5.3 Stages in the disciplinary procedure

The ACAS Code describes four stages in the disciplinary procedure.

1 For a minor offence, a **verbal warning** or admonishment should suffice. In practice, it is prudent to record that such a warning has been issued.

2   For repeated minor offences, or a single more serious offence, a **first written warning** may be issued, setting a timetable for improvement (indicating any help which may be given to the individual by way of training or support).

3   For repeated offences, or a serious first offence just falling short of dismissal, a **final written warning** may be given, again setting a timetable for improvement and stating that further offences of this kind or related offences may result in dismissal or other penalty such as suspension without pay (if allowed for in the contract of employment).

4   **Dismissal** is the final stage, when all previous stages have been exhausted and further offences have been committed within any final improvement period that has been set.

Summary dismissal, which is dismissal without notice, may be used only in a case of bad conduct that is so serious (gross misconduct) that it requires the employee to be removed immediately from the organization.

Activity 4 · 2 mins

Who in your organization has the authority to *dismiss* an employee and what authority do *you* have to impose disciplinary sanctions (for example, a recorded verbal warning or first written warning)?

_____

_____

_____

Your answer will vary according to the policies and procedures of your own organization.

Normally, the authority of a team leader or first line manager will be limited to issuing a verbal warning or admonition. This provides a check on employers, because it protects employees from being sacked or disciplined severely by an immediate superior who may bear a personal grudge against them. The same principle applies at every level. For example, a first line manager should not normally be dismissed by the manager to whom he or she reports without reference to a higher level of management.

5.4 Appeals procedure

To be perceived as fair within the law, an employee should have a right to appeal within a specified period (normally two days) to a senior manager.

This provides a further check on managers by offering employees an opportunity to seek an independent review of a decision that may affect their future career with the company. Employment Tribunals will take the existence of an appeals procedure into account when considering cases of unfair dismissal.

5.5 Applying disciplinary policies and procedures fairly and consistently

Employment Tribunals look to see that procedures, however reasonable they may be in *theory,* are applied fairly and consistently in *practice.* If they are not, then they will not be accepted as meeting the requirements of the law.

Activity 5 · 5 mins

An organization recently dismissed a long serving employee, Sarah Cole, for persistent lateness, after a final written warning had not brought about any improvement. She applied to an Employment Tribunal, claiming unfair dismissal, bringing two employees as witnesses, both of whom had two final written warnings on file but had not been dismissed.

How do you think the Tribunal would have found, and why?

_____

_____

_____

Almost certainly, the Tribunal would have found in Sarah's favour. This is because the procedures, though reasonable in themselves, had not been applied consistently. Sarah had been dismissed but her two colleagues had not, even though they had also received two written warnings. The records proved that the organization had not applied its own rules consistently.

6 Dealing with recognized trades unions

Under defined conditions, a trade union may apply to the Central Arbitration Committee for legal recognition. Many employers grant recognition voluntarily. In a dispute ACAS can help the parties to reach a mutually acceptable agreement.

Where a trade union has legal recognition, or has been granted representation rights by your organization, it will have the right to take up grievance and disciplinary matters on behalf of its members, initially through the local shop steward.

If you work within a unionized workplace, or are a member of a union yourself, you will know that unions can help to provide an orderly working environment. Shop stewards, safety representatives and union officials are usually well trained in the organization's policies and procedures and the laws that underpin them. They can help you in your efforts to manage employees fairly and consistently.

6.1 Members of trades unions without legal recognition or representation rights

You may work with people who are members of a trade union that is not recognized by your employer and that does not have representation rights for employees who belong to it.

They may belong to an unrecognized union because of the benefits it offers, or they may have stayed in a union which was recognized by a former employer.

A union that is not 'recognized', in the legal sense, does not have a legal right to take up issues on behalf of the employee. This is true even if a number of employees belong to it, unless it has been granted representation rights specifically to act in individual cases of grievance or discipline.

You need to be sure what situation members of your team are in concerning trade union rights.

7 Employment records

A prudent employer will keep accurate and up-to-date records of individual employees, starting from the very beginning of employment.

The records should always include an acknowledgement from the employees that they have received a copy of the Employee Handbook and have had its contents explained to them.

For any disciplinary process to withstand scrutiny by an Employment Tribunal, there must be accurate records of disciplinary actions involving every individual.

Activity 6

5 mins

State, in your own words, why it is important for an employer to keep up-to-date written records of each employee's progress and conduct throughout his or her period of employment. Draw on your own experience, wherever possible, as an employee and a manager.

_____

_____

_____

You may have included issues such as the following: memories are imperfect over a period of time; employees may deny being told something (such as a disciplinary warning) if there is no written proof; an employer may claim that an employee was told something which they deny.

In practice, for most people, there will be nothing to record in a well run organization; but for those employees who cannot, or will not, comply with the organization's rules, there must be a written record of actions taken.

Similarly, there must be a record available of any grievances raised by an employee and of the action taken to try to resolve it.

The records need to comply with the requirements of the Data Protection Act.

7.1 Exit interviews

It is good practice, with their consent, to conduct an exit interview with all employees who leave of their own volition. Exit interviews can provide valuable information about the attitudes of employees since they now have nothing to lose by being frank. A record of the interview can also be valuable if they change their minds later on as to why they left the organization. This is particularly important if they go on to pursue a claim to an Employment Tribunal for unfair dismissal.

Self-assessment 1

20 mins

1   Fill in the three blanks in the following sentence.

The law impinges on many aspects of employing people, including:

a _____

b _____

c _____

2   Suggest three ways in which an employer can ensure that its employment policies are communicated effectively to all employees.

_____

_____

_____

3 _____ , _____ ,

and _____ are three of the main grounds on which

an employee can make an application to an Employment Tribunal.

4 How can well established grievance procedures help an organization manage
legally?

_____

_____

5 The main stages in a formal disciplinary procedure as recommended by ACAS
are:

1 _____

2 _____

3 _____

4 _____

6 A major principle of sound disciplinary procedures is that _____

is allowed to dismiss their _____ subordinate without reference

to a higher level of management.

7 No matter how good a disciplinary procedure is, it will not be effective legally

unless it is applied _____ and _____ .

8 Written records of disciplinary procedures used in relation to an individual

employee are essential to prove to an _____ that an

organization has acted fairly.

9 Appeal procedures are an essential part of _____

procedures if they are to be seen as fair by an _____ .

10 Membership of an employment tribunal comprises a _____

who is legally qualified; a second member with _____

and a third who has a _____ background.

Answers to questions can be found on pages 92–93.

8 Summary

■ For an organization to comply with the letter and spirit of the many laws touching on employing people, it is essential that it has:

- policies and procedures founded on best practices such as ACAS codes of practice;
- means of communicating them intelligibly to all employees, such as an Employee Handbook;
- induction training;
- employee briefing systems to keep everyone up to date with changes which will affect them;
- records of all actions taken under disciplinary procedures;
- evidence that it applies its policies fairly and consistently.

■ The four stages in the formal disciplinary procedure are:

1 verbal warning;
2 first written warning;
3 second written warning;
4 dismissal.

Session B
Managing positively

1 Introduction

In this session, we'll look at the positive aspects of leading teams to achieve a harmonious working environment. Such an environment does not come about by happy accident. It owes much to the skill and attitude of the team leader, who can make a real difference to the spirit with which a team performs and so help them to achieve the organization's standards for such key performance indicators as quality, delivery, safety, absence and staff turnover.

Team leaders work in the front line of employment relations. Signs of unhappiness, disaffection, disagreements between individuals, lack of comprehension of organizational policies and a reluctance to observe the rules and procedures that flow from them should be apparent to the team leader long before they come to the notice of senior management. Many or most problems should be resolvable at this first level, before they have had a chance to ferment into a more stubborn issue over which people may take up entrenched positions.

An Employment Tribunal is a body appointed to adjudicate on legal disputes involving unfair dismissal, victimization or discrimination in relation to race, sex, or disability.

The title of this workbook, *Managing Lawfully – People and Employment*, reflects the fact that the law is now present in the background for virtually every aspect of employment, from recruitment to resignation or retirement. Employment Tribunals, to whom aggrieved employees may eventually take their cases, can and do make awards running into many thousands of pounds where employers are held to have acted unfairly.

However, in organizations where the positive approaches described and advocated in this session are applied by team leaders, it is much less likely that managers need be concerned about the threat of employment tribunal cases, or other aspects of poor working relationships such as low morale, poor productivity, indifferent service and quality standards or, ultimately, the withdrawal of labour in unofficial or official disputes.

2 Achieving harmony at work

The dictionary defines harmony as:

> 'agreement, or concord. In music, a combination of notes which form chords of melodious sound.'

The team leader is the person who should strive to achieve this desirable condition within the team, just as the conductor of a brass band or an orchestra ensures that the sounds produced by individual players combine to produce the desired effect. Team leaders' lives are certainly much happier when an atmosphere of agreement and concord prevails.

For a conductor, there is a written score to refer to, which sets out in black and white the composer's intentions. All the players have a copy of it, can read it and are broadly committed to what the composer wishes them to do. Professional musicians have reached a defined standard of competence. This means that the conductor can be confident that all can use their instruments as required by the composer. In a military band, there is also a framework of military discipline and imposed respect for senior rank.

Activity 7 · 5 mins

List three factors from your own experience of work which can make a team leader's task more difficult than that of a military band leader or orchestra conductor.

_____

_____

_____

The factors which you have identified probably include:

■ people who aren't competent to do the job required of them;
■ individuals who are uncommitted to the company's objectives, or who don't understand them;
■ rivalries between individuals who have differing ideas about how best to do the work;
■ people who would simply prefer doing a different job;
■ individuals who don't understand what is required of them;
■ lack of respect for the team leader by one or more of the team;
■ resentment by some members who believe others aren't doing their share of the work.

If a brass band suffered from some or all of these adverse factors, how harmonious do you think its overall sound would be? Discord would prevail and the composer, if listening, would hardly recognize the work.

Activity 8

3 mins

Complete the following sentences using the words provided.

SELECTION   EARN   TRAINING   EXPLAINED   FAVOURS

1   If someone isn't competent to do the job, this is probably because of poor _____ and _____ .

2   An uncommitted employee often has not had the organization's policies _____ to them intelligibly.

3   Rivalries between individuals may arise when a team leader apparently _____ some team members by comparison with others.

4   A team leader must _____ the respect of all team members.

EXTENSION 4
Visit the Department of Trade and Industry website for useful information on employment relations.

The answers can be found on page 94.

As a team leader, you have the responsibility to ensure that none of these barriers to harmonious working exists. You may need to act directly, or by influencing your manager or other specialist managers to act.

3 Selection and training

An employee unable to do the job properly will almost certainly be unhappy, and may show signs of work-related stress. Once you recognize the problems, you should arrange whatever training and coaching is necessary to bring them up to the standard required.

The importance of induction training was stressed in Session A. Team leaders have a vital role to play in making sure new employees go through the induction process. Even if this involves some temporary inconvenience, it will help you greatly in the longer term, when employees cannot say 'Nobody told me about . . .'

If you are constantly finding team members incapable of doing the job, then you need to do something to influence the way in which they are selected. Otherwise team morale will inevitably suffer and your problems will multiply.

4 Appraising performance

Some organizations carry their staff appraisal systems through to every employee. Where this happens, it gives you the opportunity for a detailed review of an individual employee's performance. You can also find out more about what the employee thinks of your performance as a team leader.

Appraisals can be an uncomfortable experience for both parties to the interview. But, provided you are trained to carry them out and everyone knows clearly that their purpose is to help improve performance and working relationships, they should be very helpful to the quest for harmonious working.

If your organization does not have such a comprehensive appraisal system, you can still try to find a little extra time to help employees with particular problems or to support those who wish to realize their full potential within the organization.

5 Communicating with the team

You have the responsibility for implementing the organization's policies with your team – just as a conductor has to make the right sounds appear from the notes written in the music.

If team members don't understand fully what is required of them, it's your job, in the first instance, to explain what they need to do – and *why*.

Ultimately, there is a job to be done and there is no point everyone working happily together if they are not delivering what is required. If the organization is being put at risk of failure there will be a corresponding threat to the team's success.

5.1 Formal briefing systems

Some organizations use formal briefing groups, or 'tool box talks', to help put the message across. You should take full advantage of such formal structures, but never treat them as a substitute for regular, day-to-day communications on key issues with all members of your team. These issues include: quality, performance targets, safety, hygiene and housekeeping.

5.2 Listening to feedback

Communication with your team needs to be a two-way process. A potent threat to harmonious working is the feeling on behalf of an individual, or section within a team, that 'nobody listens to their concerns', perhaps about safety or perceived unfairness in the way that working rotas are arranged, or holiday dates allocated.

You need to listen to your team's problems and deal immediately with the points you believe have merit. You can either do this directly, where you have sufficient authority to do so, or through colleagues or senior managers where you need help.

5.3 'Opportunist' team briefings

Where a formal briefing system isn't in place, you may be able to find 'opportunist' occasions to talk to your team as a group. This could be at the beginning of a shift, at the end of the working week, during maintenance breaks or when the computer system has crashed. However you do it – and one of the reasons you were appointed will have been your ability to use initiative – *talking* to your team together will help get them all *working* together.

Also it will help you to sense any rivalries or unhappiness that could sow the seeds of discord if you don't deal with them promptly.

6 Earning respect from the team

In all organizations, real respect has to be *earned*. Even in the military sphere, it doesn't really come from having a sergeant's stripes or a lieutenant's 'pips'.

Activity 9

5 mins

Take the following list of factors and rate them in order of importance for earning respect from your team (from 1 = most important to 10 = least important).

Factor	Your rating
Knowing the job	
Listening to what team members think	
Setting an example, for example, in timekeeping and attendance	
Being available to talk to individuals	
Sticking to what you say	
Tackling individuals' poor performance	
Encouraging people who show promise	
Helping people who have particular temporary problems and needs	
Walking the job at least once each day or shift	
Treating everyone with respect and courtesy	

This Activity is designed to make you think hard, and there is no single 'right' answer.

In practice, all ten factors are important in a team leader's endeavours to gain respect. Every factor listed begins with a verb, a 'doing word', implying the need for *action* by the leader.

The emphasis will change from time to time, but any team leader will need to *act* positively in every way to earn the respect they need.

Activity 10 ·

Take the ten factors listed in Activity 9 and test your own leadership style candidly against them.

■ Identify any areas to which you believe that you need to give more attention.
■ Plan any actions that you need to take to address those areas, either on your own or with assistance from your own manager or others within your organization.

If it helps, imagine you work for a manager who does the *opposite* of the ten positive actions in the way that he or she manages *you*.

Areas needing attention

_____

_____

_____

Action you need to take

_____

_____

_____

7 Motivating and monitoring

There are many approaches to the motivation of individuals and teams at work. Your organization may use several of them, and you may have experience of others elsewhere.

The aims of all the well-founded approaches are to:

■ recognize and seek out the contributions of individuals;
■ encourage all team members to accept ownership of the organization's goals;
■ ensure that the task, whatever it may be, is completed consistently to the defined standards and on time.

7.1 Monitoring effectiveness

All motivational approaches need to be monitored for their effectiveness in a particular situation. Probably the simplest and most telling way to do so is to measure the outcomes from the approach being used. This is illustrated by the following case study, involving a team working in a busy despatch department.

7.2 Case study

Six months ago the despatch department of an office stationery supplier was re-organized because performance levels were unsatisfactory. The team leader's role was re-designated as 'facilitator'. The 11 members of the team (including the facilitator) were designated as an 'autonomous working group'. They now took joint responsibility for meeting all targets. The comparative measures for before and after the change are as follows:

Factor	Performance factors	
	Before Change	After Change
% of items delivered on time	88.9	87.6
% of items returned damaged (inadequate packaging)	3.6	3.8
Customer complaints per week (average)	17	16
Number of accidents reported per week (average for 6 month period)	0.5	0.75
Sickness absence per employee (days per month)	0.63	0.94
Overtime payment rate hours worked (average per week)	2.9	3.9
Number of employees who left (total for six months)	3	5
Number of disciplinary proceedings begun	7	1
Equipment availability (%)	87.4	95.9

The organization's main stated aims when the new system came in were:

1   to deliver to our customers on the next day in 96% of cases with less than 1% of damage due to inadequate packaging;

2   to stabilize levels of sickness absence, overtime working and staff turnover;

3   to re-establish disciplinary standards and reduce accident levels due to indiscipline.

Activity 11 · *15 mins*

Study the data and then state how closely you believe each of the three stated objectives have been met by the new working system introduced to re-motivate the department.

_____

_____

_____

Provide a short written summary giving your overall assessment of the situation now (better? worse? little or no change?) and the reasons you infer may be contributing to it.

_____

_____

_____

As with most real-life situations in management, there is no 'right' answer to the questions you were asked. What is plain from the data presented is that the organization has failed in most areas, sometimes significantly, to meet its stated objectives. You will have noted that:

■   sickness absence, accident rates and overtime working have all increased sharply;

- the number of disciplinary actions initiated has dropped sharply, which may show that no-one is now prepared to take responsibility, given the poor performance levels;
- staff turnover has increased, itself usually a symptom of poor morale, possibly good employees are leaving because of the undisciplined atmosphere;
- the former team leader's job title has changed, but was any training, coaching or management support offered to help with the transition?

If the 'proof of the pudding is in the eating', then it is apparent that the switch to a self-regulating group has not worked as intended by any *objective* measure.

The remaining team members may be very happy and taking home more overtime pay, but, happy or not, they are failing to deliver the service levels required, and that could imperil their jobs and the company's future in the competitive market for office supplies, where service is everything.

One of the few things to have improved is the availability percentage for equipment; so the team is being given the tools, but failing to do the job.

7.3 Using objective measures

Not everything is measurable, but it makes sense to use objective measures wherever reasonably practicable to assess the success, or otherwise, of motivational techniques.

Once you have assessed the outcomes from the technique, as shown in the case study, you can then look at the *process* by which it was implemented to see where it is succeeding (or failing) to deliver.

Sticking with our case study, it seems apparent that insufficient preparation, training and support management was received from more senior managers to implement a system that has been used successfully in many workplaces.

Probably also, the long-term benefits to the team and its facilitator were explained insufficiently clearly. The one thing senior management *had* delivered on was improving the efficiency of the equipment provided.

The 'before change' data show clearly that there had been problems with service performance and damage, plus a high number of formal disciplinary actions (considering there are only ten employees, excluding the team leader).

Some of this implies negative attitudes and a lack of commitment to the organization and its objectives. There is no doubt that the problems needed to be faced, using a combination of the approaches already described in this session and stressing *why* there is need for change and improvement.

Until people accept that there *is* a problem, they are very unlikely to give their support to any system or technique intended to *solve* or *lessen* it.

8 Recognising and resolving conflict situations

8.1 Eliminating the negative

An old pop song counsels listeners to 'accentuate the positive . . . that's what gets results'.

Up to this point this session has concentrated on the positive aspects of managing. However, the real world of work is not Utopian, and negative factors arise even in the best run organizations.

The same old song advises also that you should 'eliminate the negative' so we will now tackle some of the thornier problems.

8.2 The potential for conflict

The reasons for potential conflict can be many and various, and they aren't always rational.

Problems away from work

Team members may simply not get on, for reasons that have nothing to do with work. For example:

- they may support different football teams;
- they may have a dispute outside work that you know nothing about.

Losing sympathy with the organization

Individuals may become out of sympathy with the organization. Imagine someone who has:

- stopped smoking, but still works for a cigarette company;
- lost a friend or relative in a road accident, but works for a car distributor;
- become a strict vegetarian, but works for a shop selling some animal products.

Bullying and harassment

EXTENSION 5
You can find out more about how to handle bullying from ACAS.

What begins as a bit of harmless teasing can escalate into bullying, with serious implications if it is not tackled early.

Likewise, sexual, racial or religious harassment may begin as what the instigator regards as 'harmless fun' the victim may be thought of as 'thin skinned' or 'lacking a sense of humour'.

Custom and practice

Years ago, people often underwent initiation rites when completing an apprenticeship. Nowadays, many of these would be frowned upon and, if imposed against the victim's will, could lead to an Employment Tribunal.

Such initiation rites may be long-established custom and practice in a place of work, and can be a potential source of conflict.

Other possible examples include workplaces where it has been the practice for years to watch adult films in the relaxation area. A new employee may find this objectionable or even threatening.

Similarly, established employees may have broken many safety rules in order to finish early on Friday afternoons. Perhaps the previous team leader turned a blind eye, so when you tackle the issue, conflict could ensue.

Such sub-cultures can, if unchecked, eventually completely usurp your authority as a manager.

8.3 The team leader as 'intelligence officer'

Any of these situations – and you may think of many others – could cause conflict. It could arise either within your team, or between a member of the team and yourself as the representative of management policies and objectives.

If you are 'walking the job' regularly and talking to everyone in your team daily, or more often, you will soon start to feel the bad vibrations that emanate from various situations.

Activity 12

Look at the following signals given by members of a team, and write down what action you would take as their team leader. Then add up to three further signals from your own experience and say what you *actually* did.

Signal 1:
Hassan and Victor always make a point of sitting a long way apart in the tea room. They have been seen to 'jostle' each other when clocking in.

Action:

_____

_____

_____

Signal 2:
Four new employees have all left one section within a few days of starting work. According to the section 'old hands' they didn't seem to fit in.

Action:

_____

_____

_____

Signal 3:
Graffiti derogatory to an ethnic group has begun to appear in the washroom. No-one will admit responsibility.

Action:

_____

_____

_____

Signal 4:
A new employee has asked for a 'sub' against her wages and is very vague about why she needs it.

Action:

_____

_____

_____

Signal 5:

_____

Action:

_____

_____

_____

Signal 6:

_____

Action:

_____

_____

_____

Signal 7:

_____

Action:

_____

_____

_____

You may have made suggestions along the following lines.

1   Talk to Hassan and Victor individually. Get them to open up by using open questions beginning with 'How', 'What', 'Where', 'When', 'Why' and 'Who'. For example, you could say 'How do you think Victor is settling in to the team?' 'What does Hassan think of the new quality procedures?' Once you have a reasonable idea of what the bad feeling is about, you can try to resolve the cause. If it is a work-related problem (such as working rotas), you may be able to resolve it yourself. If not, you can try to help them see that prejudices or disputes outside work cannot be allowed to affect your team's morale and performance.

2   Question the 'old hands' as to why and how the four newcomers didn't fit in. Look for any evidence of a sub culture – card schools, working practices outside the rules, prejudices to do with working with particular groups. If they are freezing the newcomers out, you will need to take positive steps to restore standards throughout your team.

3   Gather any evidence available from the cleaning staff and other departments. Talk to your team members individually and as a group, making it plain that this is unacceptable behaviour – whoever is doing it – and that it could represent serious misconduct. Try to discover what is at the root of it (it may be nothing directly to do with race), and if necessary encourage members to discuss the underlying issues with you, explaining that only then can you try to resolve them.

4   Ask the employee tactfully why she needs the sub, explaining that if it is for purely personal reasons it can be dealt with under the organization's normal rules. However, if someone is demanding money from her, as a sort of commission or entry fee, that could be gross misconduct and might land the person in serious trouble if they persist in the demand. If the problem persists you could encourage her to use the confidential grievance procedure, and you may eventually need assistance from your manager.

The last three signals, which you have described from your own experience, should have illustrated the benefits of constantly monitoring what goes on in your team, and taking immediate action to deal with any problems that arise.

9 Resolving conflict

In some cases, you may need help to resolve conflict situations. However, if you attune yourself to *recognizing* the signals of conflict and becoming a figure of trust for your team members, many of the situations may resolve themselves before you need additional help.

9.1 Somebody must pay . . . or must they?

It is often said that we now live in a blame culture, with lawyers eager to find any offences which may result in substantial compensation for the victim and sizeable fees for them.

Whether or not that is true for society at large, you should *not* encourage such a culture to develop within your team.

Just as the best and chief reason for investigating accidents is to prevent them happening again, so the chief reason for resolving conflict should be to achieve more harmonious working relationships and a generally more pleasant, positive atmosphere in which to work. Fear of being blamed or disciplined unjustly will make it much harder to reach the root of any problem, which is no good to anyone.

You need to be seen as:

- a leader who can be trusted to act, first and foremost, in the interests of fairness and improved working relationships for the future;
- someone committed to resolving the problem, wherever possible, to the satisfaction of all parties *without* seeking to apportion blame as though in a court of law.

9.2 The ideal 'win–win' situation . . .

Most of the time, your aim should be to achieve a settlement that allows all parties to believe that they have achieved something from the negotiation. For example, it might be possible to encourage some give and take over issues such as working rotas, overtime allocation, tea breaks or out-of-hours parking spaces in order to achieve the desirable 'win–win' outcome.

9.3 ... and the realities of the law

However, there can be no compromize over some issues, including those where safety or other working practices are concerned that conflict with the law.

An organization cannot condone practices that are illegal, and you can have no authority to do so on its behalf.

If another employee's safety or employment rights were to be compromized by your complicity, then the matter could end up being resolved by an Employment Tribunal, with inevitable negative results for the organization and for you.

10 Grievance procedures

These procedures were introduced in Session A and can have a beneficial part to play in resolving potential conflicts of many kinds.

Activity 13 · 3 mins

Give three or four examples of grievances that employees might wish to raise. One example you might think of is being bullied by other employees.

_____

_____

_____

_____

There could be many items on your list, including:

- being passed over continually for promotion;
- never being offered overtime (*or* required to do too much overtime);
- sexual or racial harassment;
- being given all the 'rotten work', for example, piece work with limited earnings potential;
- being required to do work offensive to religious beliefs;
- being ignored by colleagues ('sent to Coventry') for working too hard.

There can be no definitive list for grievances, and one person will shrug off something that another will regard as a major problem.

It is unlikely that every aggrieved employee will be satisfied with the solution available through following the formal grievance procedures.

Some grievances may be more imaginary than real, while others may be impossible to resolve without changing the entire organization, which is probably impractical.

Even so, having an official channel for grievances may be a useful safety valve to those involved.

10.1 Positive use of grievance procedure

The very existence of a grievance procedure encourages people to use it, provided that there is evidence that the organization takes it seriously. Some problems are solvable, given goodwill and trust.

It is far better for employees to feel that they can do something, rather than 'nursing' their grievance and perhaps eventually leaving the organization and claiming constructive dismissal before an Employment Tribunal. If a Tribunal hearing arises, having and following a formal, recorded grievance procedure shows that your organization has tried to help employees to resolve their problems within its own structure and the law.

10.2 Role of the first line manager and team leader

First line managers and team leaders are the most likely first point of contact, and should be the people best able to resolve problems quickly. You need to show staff that you will try to resolve their genuine concerns without delay.

As with many aspects of management, grievance handling is more art than science. The approaches advocated in this session, used conscientiously, will help you to:

■ keep the number of perceived grievances raised to a minimum;
■ deal sympathetically and objectively with those that reach you;
■ prevent many or most of them escalating into a crisis that diverts attention from the main objectives agreed for your team.

Self-assessment 2

10 mins

1 Name four actions that a team leader can take to help earn the respect and trust of the team.

_____

_____

_____

_____

2 The use of team briefing will ensure that everyone in the team knows _____ is required of them and that everyone gets the _____ message.

3 Team leaders need to be good _____ and able to _____ on what they hear when necessary.

4 Team leaders should ensure that all new team members go through an _____ process when they first join the organization.

5 Assigning _____ to one party or another is always _____ in resolving conflict situations.

6 Give three examples of an individual employee's concerns which a well-founded grievance procedure might help resolve.

_____

_____

_____

7 Custom and practice may be evidence of sub-cultures which, if not addressed, can _____ your authority as a leader.

8 Name one potential benefit from using a formal appraisal system;

■ for the appraiser;
■ for the person being appraised.

For the appraiser:

_____

For the person being appraised:

_____

Answers to these questions will be found on page 93.

11 Summary

- Harmony is the desirable condition where people work together cheerfully and give of their best to help you achieve organizational objectives.

- First line managers can make a major contribution to achieving good working relationships.

- The selection, induction, initial and continuing training of staff are vital aspects of developing both individual and team performance and high morale.

- Briefing, formal or informal, is a powerful tool that you can use to ensure that all team members know what is required of them and get the same message.

- Communication is a two way process – team leaders need to listen attentively and take note of what they hear.

- Respect will be earned by treating people with respect and courtesy and applying appropriate management techniques.

- It is essential to monitor the effectiveness of motivational approaches and make adjustments to suit the organizational circumstances.

- First line managers should recognize actual and potential conflict situations and resolve them wherever possible.

- Attributing blame is as unhelpful in conflict situations as it is when investigating accidents. The object in both areas should be to prevent recurrence of the problem.

- Grievance procedures, properly used and respected, can be a positive force for resolving situations that could lead to conflict.

- While the law is always there in the background of all employment practices, managing positively will keep you in step with it and keep you away from potentially disastrous Employment Tribunal hearings.

Session C
Discipline

1 Introduction

Any group of people is much more effective when it works as a team. As a team leader in your own workplace you will no doubt appreciate that fact.

Without discipline, teamwork can easily break down. If individual members of a team are refusing to pull their weight or cannot perform to the standards required of them, then the overall effectiveness of the group suffers. Other members, seeing that they are doing more than their colleagues, will either decide to take it easy themselves, or become angry that work is not being shared evenly.

Remember, discipline is not about punishment. It is about resolving problems at work in as fair a manner as possible. In the interests of fairness, there should always be clear rules about the way that disciplinary problems are dealt with. In this Session we'll examine each of the stages in the process of maintaining discipline.

2 The purpose of discipline

This workbook concentrates on practical ways of handling discipline. However, before we start we should try to define what discipline is for.

Activity 14

Write down **two** purposes of discipline at work.

_____

_____

_____

_____

See whether you agree with the following arguments.

Discipline at work has four main objectives:

- safety;
- fairness;
- prosperity of the organization;
- compliance with a contract.

2.1 Safety

Someone entering a workplace for the first time won't necessarily be able to know how to behave. In particular, he or she probably won't be aware of the dangers of that workplace, and so won't be safe until told about the hazards and the means of protection against those hazards. Employees who ignore safety rules, or who indulge in fighting or drinking at work, for example, may endanger others.

2.2 Fairness

People may under-perform in various ways which impose extra work and responsibility on their colleagues. Sometimes this may be conduct such as lateness or absenteeism, but it may also be that they cannot meet the standards required for output or quality. Fairness must be seen to flow from the employer, evidenced by proper training or re-training, and from the first line manager through offering appropriate support. In return, individuals must observe the rules and ask for help if they cannot meet the standards set.

2.3 Prosperity of the organization

For an organization to prosper, it will need the vast majority of employees to obey the rules and meet the agreed performance standards for the greater part of the time. Employees who fall short in either respect should be given support and the opportunity to improve in whatever respect they are failing. For the few who cannot, or will not, improve, then the formal disciplinary procedures exist to offer a final series of opportunities to do so before they must be dismissed in the interests of their colleagues and the other stakeholders in the organization.

2.4 Compliance with a contract

Under the terms of the contract of employment, the employer provides facilities and resources, such as training, supervision and payment for agreed work done. In return, the employees commit themselves to meeting agreed standards of conduct and performance once their training is completed.

Discipline at work should work for the benefit of the organization and everyone who works in it.

And when dealing with a disciplinary offence, there is one guiding principle:

The main aim is improvement in performance, not punishment.

3 Rules

If there is to be discipline at work, there has to be a set of rules. Rules help to determine the standards of conduct expected from employees.

This is important because people need to know what is expected of them.

Everyone needs to know what the rules are, and the reasons for the rules.

Activity 15

3 mins

Note down **two** or **three** examples of the rules that affect the people at your place of work.

_____

_____

_____

Typical of the kinds of rule that are found in work organizations are:

- rules about timekeeping;
- rules about absence;
- rules about health and safety;
- rules about using company facilities;
- rules about who does what;
- rules about what constitutes gross misconduct.

The law of the land applies at work as well as outside it, even though the list of rules drawn up by an organization won't normally remind employees of that fact. It goes without saying that it is a disciplinary offence to steal or to damage property, for instance.

It's obviously preferable for the rules of an organization to be written down.

Activity 16

4 mins

Even if the rules are written down, there can be problems in communicating the rules to all employees.

Note **one** such problem, and say how it could be overcome.

_____

_____

_____

_____

Problems can arise with:

- new employees, who aren't familiar with the accepted and safe ways to behave in the new workplace. They need to have the rules explained to them – it usually isn't good enough simply to provide a copy of the rules, especially where safety is concerned. Explaining the rules forms part of an induction programme;
- people who don't speak English as their first language. You must take steps to make sure the rules are understood. If you don't speak the particular language yourself, you will need help from more senior management or the human resources department to make sure you act effectively;
- young people, who don't have experience of working life. Again, it may fall to you to ensure that a young person fully understands the rules and why they have to be followed.

4 Dealing with offences

What is a disciplinary offence?

Activity 17 · 4 mins

Let's start by thinking about the disciplinary offences you may have had to deal with at work, or those you may have heard about.

Note down some examples of disciplinary offences. Try to think of **three** or **four**. An example is stealing.

_____

_____

_____

_____

Here are some disciplinary offences:

- fighting;
- verbal abuse;
- lateness;
- abusing company equipment;
- disobeying a reasonable instruction;
- stealing;
- smoking in a non-smoking area;
- horse-play.

You may have come up with offences not on this list. The list of disciplinary offences is as long as our imaginations can make it.

However, all these offences involve one thing:

all disciplinary matters involve a breach of rules or failure to meet agreed standards of work.

If we want to deal with disciplinary matters in a consistent and fair way, we need to:

- know what the standards and **rules** are; and
- have a well-designed **procedure** for implementing them.

Let's think about the steps a manager or team leader needs to take when there has been a suspected disciplinary offence.

Activity 18 · 3 mins

Suppose someone in another team stops you in the corridor and says something like:

'Two of your blokes left an hour early last night. That's not the first time. I don't think it's fair. What are you going to do about it?'

What is the **first** thing you would do?

_____

_____

Perhaps you agree that the first thing to be done when a breach of the rules is reported is to:

find out the facts.

Until you've looked into the matter thoroughly to see if the accusation has any truth in it, you aren't in a position to make any judgements.

Activity 19

3 mins

What might you do next, assuming you found out that **two** of your workteam had left early without permission?

_____

_____

_____

_____

You might do one of a number of things. You could for instance:

- have a quiet word with them;
- give them a warning about their behaviour;
- take the matter further and start formal disciplinary proceedings.

Before taking the matter forward, you need to determine whether you have the necessary authority to act. If you haven't, or are not sure, it is imperative to consult your own manager before going too far along the disciplinary road.

Any formal procedures usually involve a **disciplinary interview**. This gives the people accused a chance to state their version of the facts. Then you would be able to come to a considered judgement about what penalty you should impose – if any.

Once you decided on the action to be taken, you'd need to record the information and keep an eye on things from that point on.

We can sum up all these steps in the form of a diagram. We'll be using this diagram as we go through the rest of this part of the workbook.

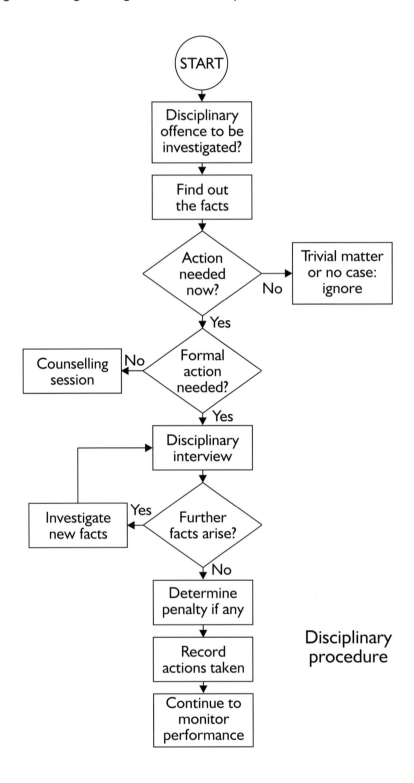

Disciplinary procedure

Activity 20

20 mins

S/NVQ C15.2

This Activity may provide the basis of appropriate evidence for your S/NVQ portfolio. If you are intending to take this course of action, it might be better to write your answers on separate sheets of paper.

1 Explain how well you ensure that your team members are kept informed of the organization's disciplinary procedures.

_____

_____

_____

2 What actions do you intend to take to make them better informed? (Learn more yourself? Hold a team meeting? Talk to individuals? Or what other actions?)

_____

_____

_____

3 How confident are you that the contributions you make to implementing disciplinary and grievance procedures are consistent with your organization's values and policies?

_____

_____

_____

4 If you are less than totally confident about this, what actions will you take? (Talk to your manager? Talk to the Human Resources department? Some other action?)

_____

_____

_____

Record below the result of the actions taken in 2 and 4 above.

_____

_____

_____

_____

_____

5 Following the procedures

EXTENSIONS 6, 7, 8
and 9
ACAS has produced
several useful
publications on
disciplinary and grievance
procedures.

As all organizations have to cope with disciplinary problems, most of them have developed systematic procedures for handling them.

A **disciplinary procedure** is a set of written guidelines to help everyone at work – managers, team leaders, other employees and shop stewards – to deal with disciplinary matters.

Activity 21   5 mins

Imagine that a member of your team is failing to meet the standards set for output performance and quality. In your opinion, it is a serious matter and has continued for some time despite informal approaches from you. It merits a first written warning.

How would you act if the team member concerned were:

A long-serving employee, with a previously unblemished record

_____

_____

A shop steward

_____

_____

An employee who has had other written warnings, all now time-expired, for unrelated matters

_____

_____

A young employee who is your second cousin

_____

_____

An employee of West Indian or Irish origin

_____

_____

Your answer should be that you would act the same way in any of the situations described, based on your assessment of the facts.

To appear fair to an Employment Tribunal, the procedures must be implemented in a consistent way. Everyone must be treated in the same way for the same offence – and all team leaders and managers must act in the same way whatever department they work in.

It makes a great deal of sense to make notes of what is said and done for future reference. Tell people that you will be doing so, and explain that you are doing it simply to ensure that there is an accurate record of what has been said. This will be to everyone's benefit.

The following extracts from an example of a good disciplinary procedure is taken with permission from _Discipline at Work – The ACAS Advisory Handbook_ and reflects the ACAS Code of Practice relating to disciplinary practice and procedures in employment.

5.1 Sound procedures

(1) Purpose and scope

This procedure is designed to help and encourage all employees to achieve and maintain standards of conduct, attendance and job performance. The company rules (a copy of which is displayed in the office) and this procedure apply to all employees. The aim is to ensure consistent and fair treatment for all.

Notice that the procedure starts by stating:

- **what** the procedure is for;
- **where** the procedure can be seen;
- **to whom** it applies.

(2) Principles

a) No disciplinary action will be taken against an employee until the case has been fully investigated.
b) At every stage in the procedure the employee will be advised of the nature of the complaint against him or her and will be given the opportunity to state his or her case before any decision is made.
c) At all stages the employee will have the right to be accompanied by a shop steward, employee representative or work colleague during the disciplinary interview.

Activity 22 · 3 mins

Why is it good practice to allow someone who is under investigation to be represented by a union official or a colleague?

_____

_____

_____

_____

_____

As you may have answered, having a union official or a friend of the alleged offender present can help to ensure there is 'fair play', and that the case is fully understood by the individual.

To continue with the ACAS example procedure:

    d) No employee will be dismissed for the first breach of discipline except in the case of gross misconduct when the penalty will be dismissal without notice or payment in lieu of notice.

(We'll discuss what is meant by 'gross misconduct' shortly.)

    e) An employee will have the right to appeal against any disciplinary penalty imposed.

    f) The procedure may be implemented at any stage if the employee's alleged misconduct warrants such action.

Activity 23

3 mins

Point (e) above is another 'essential ingredient' of a good disciplinary procedure.

Can you think of **one** reason why it is so important to allow an appeal against a penalty?

_____

_____

You may agree that allowing the right of appeal:

■ helps to make sure that justice is done;
■ reduces the possibility that someone will be harshly punished due to personal bias or animosity;
■ in the case of a dispute over the decision, allows fresh minds to be brought in.

Now we come to the main part of the procedure (which we looked at briefly in Session A). Read the following extract carefully and note that:

■ There are a number of stages. (As was stated in the principles above, the procedure may be entered at any stage – it doesn't have to be followed step by step.)
■ Each stage is a more serious step than the one before.

(3) The Procedure

Minor faults will be dealt with informally but where the matter is more serious the following procedure will be used:

Stage 1 – Oral warning

If conduct or performance does not meet acceptable standards the employee will normally be given a formal **oral warning**. He or she will be advised of the reason for the warning, that it is the first stage of the disciplinary procedure and of his or her right of appeal. A brief note of the oral warning will be kept but will be spent after ... months, subject to satisfactory conduct and performance.

Stage 2 – Written warning

If the offence is a serious one, or if a further offence occurs, a **written warning** will be given to the employee by the first line manager. This will give details of the complaint, the improvement required and the timescale. It will warn that action under Stage 3 will be considered if there is no satisfactory improvement and will advise of the right of appeal. A copy of this written warning will be kept by the first line manager but it will be disregarded for disciplinary purposes after ... months subject to satisfactory conduct and performance.

Stage 3 – Final written warning or disciplinary suspension

If there is still a failure to improve and conduct or performance is still unsatisfactory, or if the misconduct is sufficiently serious to warrant only one written warning but insufficiently serious to justify dismissal (in effect both first and final written warning), a **final written warning** will normally be given to the employee. This will give details of the complaint, will warn that dismissal will result if there is no satisfactory improvement and will advise of the right of appeal. A copy of this final written warning will be kept by the first line manager but it will be spent after ... months (in exceptional cases the period may be longer) subject to satisfactory conduct and performance.

Alternatively, consideration will be given to imposing a penalty of a disciplinary suspension without pay for up to a maximum of five working days.

Stage 4 – Dismissal

If conduct or performance is still unsatisfactory and the employee still fails to reach the prescribed standards, **dismissal** will normally result. Only the appropriate senior manager can take the decision to dismiss. The employee will be provided, as soon as reasonably practicable, with written reasons for dismissal, the date on which employment will terminate and the right of appeal.

Activity 24 · 4 mins

Answer the following questions about the procedure above by circling the appropriate box.

1   Would every minor offence have to be taken through the procedure above?

| YES | NO |

2   In which stages do the warnings given become spent or disregarded after a period of time?

| 1 | 2 | 3 | 4 |

3   After which stages does the employee have a right of appeal?

| 1 | 2 | 3 | 4 |

4   At which stages are the warnings written down?

| 1 | 2 | 3 | 4 |

5   At which stages does the employee receive a written document?

| 1 | 2 | 3 | 4 |

The answers to this activity can be found on page 94–95.

Now let's deal with what is meant by 'gross misconduct'.

Activity 25 · 3 mins

Stealing would be classified as 'gross misconduct'. List **four** other disciplinary offences that you would expect to come into this category.

_____

_____

_____

_____

Let's see what ACAS suggest as examples of offences normally regarded as gross misconduct:

- theft, fraud or deliberate falsification of records;
- fighting, or assault on another person;
- deliberate damage to company property;
- serious incapability through alcohol or being under the influence of illegal drugs;
- serious negligence which causes unacceptable loss, damage or injury;
- serious acts of insubordination.

There isn't always universal agreement about what constitutes gross misconduct, and your organization may have different ideas.

One survey of British companies and local authorities found that gambling was considered by different organizations to be:

- a minor disciplinary offence;
- a major disciplinary offence;
- gross misconduct.

The procedure that we have discussed is just one example of a disciplinary procedure that could be used by an organization, and is intended as a model for a company writing its own procedure.

> Your own organization will probably have its own procedure. That's the one you have to follow.

6 Finding out the facts

The start of our disciplinary procedure diagram shows the first step to be taken:

Read the following case and then think about what further information you would need.

Activity 26

Mrs Jones, who works in the offices at her company, one day spends some time going round the other staff collecting money for a local hospital.

Those are all the facts as you know them. You are asked to decide whether Mrs Jones has committed a disciplinary offence by doing this.

What other information would you need to know, before making your judgement?

Jot down **four** questions you would ask.

_____

_____

_____

_____

Your questions may be included here.

- How long did Mrs Jones take to make her collection?
- What prompted her to do it?
- Has she or anyone else in the organization done this sort of thing before?
- Is there a well-known management rule about what she did?
- Is Mrs Jones's general record a good one?
- Is it important that she did not leave her desk?
- Did she get permission to make the collection?

When we find out the answers to these kind of questions, it becomes possible to decide about the case.

Here are two possible sets of circumstances.

Activity 27

6 mins

Mrs Jones works in the wages department. On Monday morning, she cleared up her work, and then went round her colleagues in the department to collect money for the purchase of equipment at a local hospital. She made this collection during an extended coffee break, taking about 45 minutes in all. The first person Mrs Jones collected from was her office first line manager. Everybody in the office knew that Mrs Jones's husband had been treated for cancer at the local hospital. It was also true that other people had collected for charities in the past.

Is this a disciplinary offence? | YES | | NO |

What (briefly) are the reasons for your decision?

_____

_____

_____

Mrs Jones works as a receptionist at a local company. One Wednesday morning she repeatedly left the reception area unattended while visiting other offices to collect money. One way and another, the collection had taken most of the morning. Mrs Jones tried to keep well clear of the office manager. She was collecting for the sports and social fund at the hospital where her husband works. She also collects every week for the football pools, and management had already warned her about the time she was taking on this.

Is this a disciplinary offence? | YES | | NO |

What (briefly) are the reasons for your decision?

_____

_____

_____

Compare your answers with the response given on page 95.

The discussion following this Activity leads to the conclusion that:

it is important to make sure that as much relevant information as possible is collected about each case.

It is also important that this is done promptly, before memories of the incident fade.

One formula that can help us collect information thoroughly is the '5W' formula.

6.1 The 5W formula

This formula consists of five questions:

| WHO? | WHEN? | WHAT? | WHERE? | WHY? |

Let's look at them one at a time.

- ## Who?

Disciplinary offences always involve people so we need to ask:

- **Who** was involved?
- **Who** were the witnesses?
- **Who** are the first line managers involved?
- **Who** is the trade union representative?

- ## When?

It is always important to know when an incident happened. A whole argument can be destroyed if the wrong time or day is written down. For example, if the incident is mistakenly thought to have taken place on a Wednesday afternoon, and then the person under investigation is subsequently able to prove he or she was somewhere else at the time, the whole case collapses.

It is especially important to know whether the incident happened inside or outside working hours.

- ## What?

Before any action can be contemplated, it is obviously vital to know exactly what happened. This is seldom as easy as it sounds. In many disciplinary cases there are likely to be different versions of the same event, especially where the misconduct is serious enough for dismissal. This is where your judgement comes in.

- ## Where?

Establishing where a disciplinary offence took place is important for the record. For instance, smoking may be allowed in the canteen, but not on the petrol station forecourt. If one of your team commits an offence in another section, another first line manager may have to be involved in the investigation.

- ## Why?

The final question is to ask why the incident took place. The answer to this can make the difference between whether it is treated as a disciplinary case or not.

In asking **why**, we should remember two things:

- why did the incident happen at that time or place?
- why did it involve that particular person?

Activity 28 · 4 mins

The Cartwheel Company is a medium-sized firm operating three shifts. The shop floor is divided into a number of different sections, and normally two first line managers are on the night shift.

For two weeks now, one first line manager has been off sick and no proper cover has been arranged. Towards the end of the night shift, Harry Davies, one of the shop floor engineers, goes to see the only first line manager available. He complains that some of the men in his unit have set up a card school, and that they are never back from breaks on time. Harry claims to represent at least four other men in the section who are all fed up with carrying the extra work created by the others never being there on time.

Use the **who**, **when**, **what**, **where** and **why** formula to investigate this matter.

Write down the questions you would want answers to, in the space below.

Who? _____

_____

When? _____

_____

What? _____

_____

Where? _____

_____

Why? _____

_____

The following are typical questions drawn out by the 5W formula:

Who?

- **Who** were the members of the alleged card school?
- **Who** were those Harry said he represents?
- **Who** were the witnesses?
- **Who** were the first line managers?
- **Who** is the trade union representative?

When?

- **When** did the alleged card school sessions take place – dates and times?
- **When** did they start and finish – dates and times?

What?

- **What** did the card school involve? (Gambling for money, or was it just for fun?)
- **What** extra work did Harry and his colleagues have to do?
- **What** is the past record of this kind of offence?

Where?

- **Where** did the card school take place? (In the canteen? On the shop floor?)

Why?

- **Why** has Harry come to you? (Has he a personal grudge which has led him to blow up a small incident out of all proportion?)
- **Why** are the card games taking place? (Is the work badly organized?)
- **Why** has the information come to you in this way? (Does supervision need to be improved?)

I hope you agree with me that the 5W formula has succeeded in raising most of the important questions about the case.

Nevertheless, when you are investigating an incident like this, you will need continually to ask yourself:

is there anything more I need to know?

7 The counselling session

Let's remind ourselves of the first part of our procedure diagram for dealing with an alleged disciplinary offence:

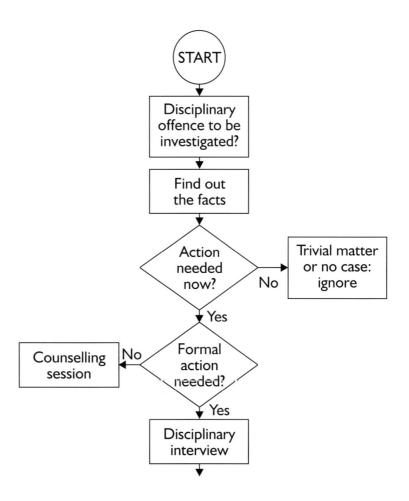

Once we have found out the facts of the case, we should know whether a disciplinary offence has been committed.

The question then arises:

Is action needed at this time?

If your judgement is that action is needed, there is another decision to be made:

Is it more appropriate to 'have a quiet word' with the offender, or is the offence serious enough to warrant a disciplinary interview?

Later in this section, we'll look into the disciplinary interview. For the moment, let's examine what's involved in a counselling session or informal discussion.

As a team leader, you are concerned to get a good performance from each member of your team, which means that breaches of discipline cannot be tolerated for long. However, you have an important role in supporting your team members. An informal discussion is an opportunity to offer your support if it is needed. If a person is under-performing, it could be due to stress and personal difficulties. A friendly approach from you can mean a lot to a harassed employee.

> Geoff Parks had been a first line manager for three years and his workteam hadn't changed much during that time.
>
> One morning, Geoff saw Jed Tarrow, one of his team, walking across the yard. He noticed Jed wasn't wearing a safety helmet.
>
> The next time Geoff saw Jed, they were both queuing at the staff canteen for lunch. They exchanged greetings and talked a while about a job Jed was working on. Then Geoff said:
>
> 'I noticed you in the yard yesterday without a helmet, Jed. That's very unlike you.'
>
> 'Sorry about that, boss. I was thinking about something else – don't know what made me forget.'
>
> 'You won't let it happen again, will you Jed? I look to you to set an example.'

You may deal with some minor breaches of discipline in a similar way yourself. Geoff knew that it would be enough to give Jed a gentle reminder. To have mentioned disciplinary procedures would not have helped here.

Compare this with the next case.

> Lila Podesta was a bright but unpredictable young woman. She worked in a large dress shop and, because she had a flair for it, the manager, Hilda Grace, allowed her to do most of the window

dressing. Lila knew she was good at this and had jokingly threatened to take her talents elsewhere if Hilda criticized her work in any way.

However, Lila 'took advantage' of her situation by repeatedly arriving to work late. Finally Hilda knew she'd have to do something. When Lila arrived one morning, half an hour late, she invited her into the office. This is what she said:

'Lila, I have a problem. Several of the other girls have complained to me that you are late to work every day, and I do nothing about it. What do you think I should do?'

'Tell me off, I suppose.'

'Lila, you are good at your job, but I think you are letting yourself down. I don't want to lose you, but wherever you work people won't put up with persistent lateness. Is there a particular problem at home?'

'Not really.'

'Well, we all have a job to do. I know that the company management won't allow me to take no action for very long. I have to ask you, to be fair to everyone else working here, to make an effort and get to work on time.'

Hilda knew that this was all she could do before invoking formal disciplinary procedures. She also knew that, if she did that, Lila would probably leave. It's the kind of difficult situation which you might have to deal with from time to time.

The rules are made for everyone. If someone breaks them, then sooner or later you have to take action.

Respect and confidentiality

One important aspect of dealing with disciplinary matters is that everyone deserves to be treated with respect, whether or not you believe them to have broken the rules.

Furthermore, all conversations between you and an individual regarding that person's conduct should be kept confidential. You may have to pass on information to those with a need to know it – your manager, perhaps, or the Human Resources department – but a breach of discipline is not something that should normally be discussed with other team members.

In many work situations, confidentiality can be difficult to maintain. When a group of people work closely together, for example, any unusual event may lead to speculation and gossip. The team leader plays a key role here, in:

- making it clear that information and views given in confidence are not for general consumption;

- setting an example by not joining in gossip about team members or other colleagues;

- not, under normal circumstances, discussing the behaviour of one team member with another;

- if possible, putting a halt to gossip by providing clear-cut information, but without disclosing anything that is not the concern of those not directly involved.

Fine lines must sometimes be trod. It is worth remembering that what counts above everything is the way the team leader behaves. If he or she can earn the respect of the team, and they know that their leader is incorruptible and trustworthy in all things, problems of this kind will tend not to arise.

Activity 29

S/NVQ C15.2

This Activity may provide the basis of appropriate evidence for your S/NVQ portfolio. If you are intending to take this course of action, it might be better to write your answers on separate sheets of paper.

Here are two sets of self-searching questions for you.

1   When dealing with matters of discipline, are you scrupulous in treating individuals with respect, whatever their suspected misdemeanour?

_____

Do you feel that others in your organization always maintain respect for the individual during disciplinary interviews and the like?

_____

Explain in what way, if at all, you intend to modify your approach in this regard. If you need evidence for your S/NVQ portfolio, you should:

■ describe one or more particular incidents in the past in some detail (omitting the names of individuals if you wish), which you thought were not handled well;

■ explain in detail how you will modify your disciplinary procedures, so that anyone accused of a disciplinary offence is treated with proper respect;

■ explain how you intend to ensure that your modified procedures will be followed. (For example, you may decide to discuss your proposals with someone from the Human Resources department, and invite them to monitor your disciplinary interviews.)

_____

_____

_____

_____

2 Does gossip tend to be rife among your team members, especially when something occurs that requires disciplinary action to be taken?

_____

_____

Explain how you usually deal with this kind of problem.

_____

_____

Now explain what you think you might do differently in this regard in the future. Again, for portfolio evidence, you must be very specific about the changes you will make, and your proposed method for ensuring these changes are followed.

_____

_____

_____

_____

_____

_____

8 Taking action

Once it is decided that formal action is to be taken, a disciplinary interview must take place.

From the procedure diagram we can see the stages to be followed:

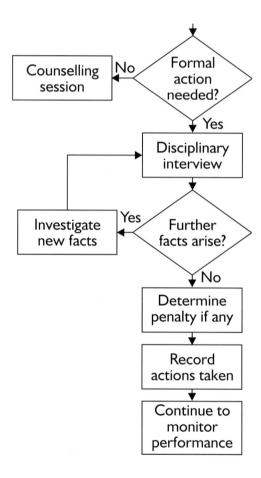

8.1 The purpose of an interview

The purposes of a disciplinary interview are to:

■ allow the employee to give his or her version of the incident;
■ ensure a full discussion, so that everyone present has a chance to hear the facts and to present any new facts;

- advise the employee of his or her rights;
- enable a fair judgement to be made so that an appropriate penalty can be imposed.

Before the interview, we have to **prepare**.

8.2 Preparing for the interview

Let's remind ourselves of the case we looked at earlier.

The Cartwheel Company is a medium-sized firm operating three shifts. The shop floor is divided into a number of different sections, and normally two first line managers are on the night shift.

For two weeks now, one first line manager has been off sick and no proper cover has been arranged. Towards the end of the night shift, Harry Davies, one of the shop floor engineers, goes to see the only first line manager available. He complains that some of the men in his unit have set up a card school, and that they are never back from breaks on time. Harry claims to represent at least four other men in the section who are all fed up with carrying the extra work created by the others never being there on time.

In order to prepare for the interview, we can apply our '5W' formula once more.

Activity 30

Use the 5W formula by answering each of the following questions. You only need give **one** answer to each question.

What is the meeting about?

_____

_____

Why do we need this meeting?

_____

_____

Who should be at the meeting?

_____

_____

Where should the meeting take place?

_____

_____

When should the meeting take place?

_____

_____

Compare your answers with the following.

■ **What** is the meeting about?

It is alleged that a card school has been started.

■ **Why** do we need this meeting?

Because this could well be a disciplinary offence.

■ **Who** should be at the meeting?

- Witnesses – to confirm the truth of the report.
- Perhaps other first line managers – to find out what they know or may have already done.
- The union representative – to keep them in the picture, and to represent the people being accused.
- The person or persons accused of the offence.

■ **Where** should the meeting take place?

A quiet area away from the workplace is much more likely to result in a satisfactory interview than a noisy area, or where others might overhear.

■ **When** should the meeting take place?

We need to give everyone involved time to prepare for the interview, so we shouldn't rush into it. We may also need to check on when the participants are available, and what times might cause the minimum disruption of work.

8.3 The interview

The interview is something that nobody looks forward to. This is all the more reason for handling it absolutely by the book.

Activity 31   3 mins

How should an interview begin?

_____

_____

_____

_____

Like any other kind of meeting, an interview should start by introducing the people present and saying what the purpose of the meeting is.

> The person alleged to be the leading member of the card school at the Cartwheel Company is called Ray Cooley. Ray has been asked to attend the interview so that we can hear what he's got to say, and eventually determine what further action should be taken.

Compare the following two ways of starting the interview:

1   The first line manager meets Ray on the shop floor.

'Look here, Ray, I know you're running a card school, so don't deny it. Nobody's getting any work done in your section and I'm sick to the back teeth with complaints. I'm giving you a written warning. Now get back to work.'

2   The first line manager arranges the interview in an office. The shop steward is present.

'Sit yourself down, Ray. You've been asked to come along today because it has been reported that you have been running a card school during the firm's time. I've checked it out and it seems you are involved, so I've called you in to have a chat about it. I think you know the other people here. You know that playing cards during working hours is against company rules, so let's hear what you've got to say.'

The first approach is likely to put Ray's back up and lead to conflict.

The second approach is much more likely to be profitable. It encourages Ray to talk and shows that no one has prejudged the case.

A courteous but firm manner is needed. It is important to encourage the employee to talk about the offence.

During the interview, it is best not to make any decisions straight away, especially where the case is a serious one.

Give yourself time to think. Adjourn the interview before you come to a conclusion.

And, most importantly:

keep a cool head – don't get emotionally involved.

8.4 The decision

Eventually a decision must be made.

Activity 32 · 2 mins

What procedure should be used to decide the further action to be taken?

Look on page 95 for feedback to this Activity.

This is how one first line manager could have ended his interview with our alleged card player, Ray Cooley.

'Right, Ray, this is the last time I want to see you in here. I'll get to the bottom of this card school affair and you'll end up being disciplined. I'm warning you not to get involved again. That's my decision, and it's final, so get out of my office.'

Activity 33 · 4 mins

Bearing in mind what the first line manager is supposed to be doing here, how many things can you find wrong with the statement above?

_____

_____

_____

_____

You may have noticed a number of problems with this first line manager's approach. Perhaps they are included here.

- It is not clear what decision – if any – has been made.
- It is not clear what sort of warning Ray has been given.
- The first line manager hasn't asked the union (or other) representative to comment.
- It is not clear what the first line manager is going to do next.
- Ray hasn't been told of his right to appeal.
- Ray hasn't been asked to respond to the statement.

I hope you agree that there are better ways to end interviews.

Such an end to a disciplinary meeting would be very unhelpful, to say the least, if the facts of it were ever to appear to before an Employment Tribunal.

Activity 34

5 mins

Read through this account of another first line manager talking to Ray Cooley, and note down the good points.

First line manager: Right, Ray, let's just sum up then. You admit that on three separate occasions – we've got the dates here – you were involved in a card school during working time. You also know that was against the work rules. Do you agree?

Ray: Yes.

Shop steward: Agreed.

First line manager: You understand that under the agreed procedure, I can give you a verbal warning for a first offence, and that is what I intend to do. Do you accept that, Ray?

Ray: Fair enough.

Shop steward: That seems fair if it's consistent with what happened to the others.

First line manager: Yes, you've been involved in all the cases, so we know we are being consistent.

OK, Ray, so this is an official verbal warning which will be confirmed to me by your union and the Human Resources department. This is the first stage of the company's disciplinary procedure. It will stay on record for six months – that will take us to the 15th of August – and if there are no more problems we will wipe the slate clean then.

If you do offend again, you should be aware that this will lead to further stages of the disciplinary procedure, and may eventually result in your being dismissed. You do have a right of appeal against this penalty, and if you want to do so, you should let Mr Renwick know by Friday.

Any final questions?

Note down the good points.

_____

_____

_____

_____

_____

Look on pages 95–96 for feedback on this activity.

8.5 After the interview

It may be tempting to heave a sigh of relief and put the matter behind you, but it is very important to complete the process thoroughly.

Activity 35   2 mins

What more is there to be done, following the disciplinary interview?

_____

_____

_____

Remember the last part of our procedure diagram:

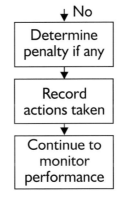

↓ No

Determine
penalty if any

↓

Record
actions taken

↓

Continue to
monitor
performance

You can see that there are two more main actions:

■ to write down the actions which have been taken

It is the job of the person holding the interview to record what took place. In some workplaces, the Human Resources department may take on this task.

■ to continue to monitor the behaviour of the person penalized for the offence

If the employee is in your team, it will be your job to keep an eye on the team member.

Let's summarize the main points to remember for the whole process.

■ **Prepare** by:
  ■ making sure you have all the information you will need;
  ■ letting everyone involved know when and where the interview is to be held;
  ■ giving the employee time to prepare.

■ **At the interview:**
  ■ introduce everyone present, explaining why they are there;
  ■ allow the employee to state his or her case;
  ■ keep the tone of the interview formal but courteous – don't lose your temper;
  ■ consider adjourning the interview to give time for a considered decision;
  ■ explain clearly what decision has been made and what further action is to be taken.

■ **After the interview:**
  ■ record the action taken;
  ■ continue to monitor the situation.

Records must be complete and accurate. According to ACAS, records should include:

■ details of the nature of any breach of disciplinary rules;
■ the action taken and the reasons for it;
■ whether an appeal was lodged;
■ its outcome and any subsequent developments.

These records should be carefully safeguarded and kept confidential.

Except in agreed special circumstances, breaches of disciplinary rules should be disregarded after a specified period of satisfactory conduct.

Remember that, if you keep records about individuals on computer, you may be subject to the Data Protection Act 1998. This obliges data users to register with the Data Protection Commissioner if the data they keep fall within the Act; failure to do this can lead to a large fine. The intent of the Act is to protect information about individuals, and to set up a mechanism whereby people can have access to information held about them.

8.6 Custom and practice

Read through the following short case study and think of yourself as being Petra Williams.

Petra Williams was about to take over as team leader in a busy warehouse. She was being shown around by her predecessor, Tony. At one point, he warned her to 'get out of the road' as a fork lift truck approached at high speed.

'That truck shouldn't be going at that speed – there's an 8 mph speed limit in here', she said

Tony smiled. 'Not on Friday afternoons there isn't', he said. 'It's 'POETS' day: 'push off early, tomorrow's Saturday'. Everyone wants to be away be four o'clock – we've always worked that way to keep everyone sweet.'

Activity 36 · · 3 mins

This is one example of 'custom and practice' at work, something which can be very hard to change and which is often quoted as a reason for breaking the rules. Can you think of three examples from your own working experience, especially something you may have been involved with before you were promoted? Examples might be:

■ using company equipment, such as faxes, telephones and email, for private use without permission;

■ borrowing equipment (drills, sanders, power saws, cameras, lap top computers) over the weekend;

■ carrying unauthorized materials or pets in company vehicles;

■ clocking (or signing) colleagues in to cover for lateness.

_____

_____

_____

As a team leader, you are best placed to know what actually happens and must be prepared to act at an early stage to prevent breaches of the rules becoming built in to the way people expect to work.

If unauthorized activities are allowed to become custom and practice, it will be much harder for you to eliminate them later. For example, imagine that the card school at the Cartwheel Company had been going for months, with managers 'turning a blind eye'; it would be much harder to take action about it.

In situations where serious or deep seated 'custom and practice' exists you will need to be tactful and may need help from your own manager or the Human Resources department.

Activity 37 · 15 mins

S/NVQ C15.2

This Activity may provide the basis of appropriate evidence for your S/NVQ portfolio. If you are intending to take this course of action, it might be better to write your answers on separate sheets of paper.

	YES	NO
Are the records you keep concerning disciplinary matters always complete and accurate?	YES	NO
Do they always include details of the nature of any breach of disciplinary rules?	YES	NO
Do they always record the action taken and the reasons for it?	YES	NO
Do they always indicate whether an appeal was lodged?	YES	NO
Do they always note the outcome and subsequent developments?	YES	NO
Are the records always carefully safeguarded and kept confidential?	YES	NO

If you answered NO to any of the questions above, explain in what way your records are deficient, or have been in the past. (For S/NVQ portfolio evidence, you should produce copies of your records if possible.)

_____

_____

_____

_____

_____

Does your organization satisfy the requirements of the Data Protection Act 1998? | YES | NO | Don't know |

Now write down any actions you plan to take as a result of your answers to these questions, to ensure that your disciplinary records conform both to the ACAS recommendations and to your organization's legal requirements. For S/NVQ portfolio evidence, you should write out very specific plans, and show how these will help your records conform. At the first opportunity, a copy of your new improved records should be included.

_____

_____

_____

_____

_____

It may not be your job to keep disciplinary records, or to ensure conformity with the law. But if your team members are involved, you will no doubt want to know that proper records are being kept, and you may be expected to input information into those records.

Self-assessment 3 ·

15 mins

1   Name one thing that all disciplinary offences involve.

_____

2   If a disciplinary offence is minor, a first line manager might decide that beginning the formal disciplinary procedure is unnecessary. What else might they do in this case?

_____

_____

3   Who benefits from there being clear rules for dealing with disciplinary offences?

_____

_____

4   Imagine that you have investigated a case and decided that formal action needs to be taken. Now you have to prepare for and hold a disciplinary interview.

   Here is a list of possible actions you might take. Pick out **seven** actions from the list and place them in the correct order, so as to describe an appropriate sequence of actions to be taken.

   a   Decide what penalty should be imposed.
   b   Decide where the meeting is to be held.
   c   Hold a counselling session.
   d   Continue to monitor performance.
   e   Decide who should be present.
   f   Introduce the participants, and state why they are there.
   g   Decide whether the case is serious enough for formal action.
   h   Sum up what's been said.
   i   Give the employee a chance to state his or her case.

_____

_____

Answers to these questions can be found on page 94.

9 Summary

- The actions involved in dealing with a disciplinary offence are:

  - find out the **facts**;
  - decide whether action is needed;
  - decide between formal action and informal action.

- If formal action is needed:

  - hold a disciplinary interview;
  - if further facts arise, investigate them;
  - determine penalty to be imposed, if any;
  - record the actions taken;
  - continue to monitor performance.

- An offence involves a breach of the rules or failure to meet standards for individual performance.

- Every well-run sizeable organization should have a written disciplinary procedure.

- First line managers should always follow procedures when dealing with discipline.

- Records about disciplinary matters must be complete and accurate. They should include: details of breach of disciplinary rules; the action taken and the reasons for it; whether an appeal was lodged; its outcome and any subsequent developments.

  These records should be carefully safeguarded and kept confidential, and may be subject to the requirements of the Data Protection Act 1998.

- To bear scrutiny by an Employment Tribunal procedures must be applied consistently to all employees within a department and by managers across all departments in the organization.

Performance
checks

1 Quick quiz

Jot down the answers to the following questions on *Managing Lawfully – People and Employment.*

Question 1   Which two documents covering the relationship between employers and employees must conform with the employment laws ?

_____

_____

Question 2   What steps may the law expect an employer to take to ensure that an individual employee understands the procedures that apply to his or her employment?

_____

_____

Question 3   Suggest three ways in which employees might break their contract of employment other than through 'gross misconduct'.

_____

_____

Question 4   What action may employees take if they believe that they have been dismissed unfairly?

_____

_____

Question 5   What rights does a recognized trade union have on behalf of its members in a disciplinary situation?

_____

_____

Question 6   Why is it important to have an appeals procedure in grievance procedures?

_____

_____

Question 7   What are the letters 'ACAS' an abbreviation for?

_____

_____

Question 8   What do you understand by 'custom and practice', and how can it affect working relationships?

_____

_____

Question 9   Why is it important to avoid assigning blame to one party or another when trying to resolve problems within your team?

_____

_____

Question 10   What do you understand by achieving a 'win–win' situation following a dispute? Are there circumstances where it is not an 'achievable outcome'?

_____

_____

Question 11   Why is it so important, legally speaking, to maintain accurate, up-to-date records of all matters affecting an individual's performance and conduct at work?

_____

_____

Question 12   There are four main objectives of discipline at work. Name **three** of them.

_____

_____

_____

Question 13   Which **three** groups of employees need special care and attention by the first line manager, to ensure that they understand the organization's disciplinary rules.

_____

_____

_____

Question 14   There are four suggested stages of a disciplinary procedure, each stage requiring a stronger action than the last. Name **three** of them.

_____

_____

_____

Question 15   List **three** offences that would normally be considered as constituting 'gross misconduct'.

_____

_____

_____

Question 16   We discussed four purposes of a disciplinary interview. List **three** of these.

_____

_____

_____

Answers to these questions can be found on pages 96–97.

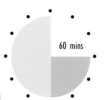

2 Workbook assessment

Read the following case incident, and then deal with the questions that follow. Write your answers on a separate sheet of paper.

Andrew Scarsbrook works in the drawing office at GHI Ltd. He has been employed for three years and has a reasonably good disciplinary record.

He usually arrives early for work – about half an hour before everybody else, and leaves half an hour early. This is no problem, as the company works a flexitime system which allows staff to clock in and out when they want to.

Doug Miller, the drawing office first line manager, has become suspicious of Andrew's work. Although he arrives half an hour early, Andrew does not often seem to have done any extra work by the time the others arrive.

Doug thinks Andrew might be working on his own account. Doug does not tell anybody, but decides one morning to turn up early himself and see what Andrew is doing.

When he arrives, Doug goes straight to Andrew's desk and asks to look at the plans he is working on. Andrew pulls something out from under the pile, but Doug can see clearly that he is working on designs for a house extension. The company's work is solely in the commercial field, so Doug confronts Andrew.

Doug: Right, I can see you are doing your own work. I've been watching you for some time. You can pack up your things and I'll take you to see Mr Blakesly in Human Resources when he arrives.

Andrew: It's only a small piece of work, Mr Miller. It's only taken me ten minutes and I haven't done it before. It won't happen again. There's no need to take this further.

Doug: I'm afraid there is. I've been watching you for some time. Doing private work in company time amounts to stealing, and that's gross misconduct. As far as I'm concerned, you are for the sack.

Later in the morning, Andrew is called in to see the Human Resources Director, David Blakesly. Mr Blakesly has already heard Doug's version of the events. He asks Andrew if he has anything to say. Andrew admits doing the private work that morning, but says again that it is the first time. In spite of this, Mr Blakesly confirms that doing private work in the firm's time is a serious disciplinary offence. He adds that he cannot afford to set a precedent by letting Andrew off the hook, so he is backing his first line manager and giving Andrew one week's notice. Andrew replies that he will be claiming unfair dismissal at an Employment Tribunal.

___

The company's disciplinary procedure is based on the ACAS procedure we looked at in the workbook. Instant dismissal is appropriate in the case of gross misconduct, and stealing is included in this category.

The procedure has been agreed with the trade union. Andrew is a member of the union.

You only need write one or two sentences in answer to each question.

1   What alternatives were open to Doug?

2   What alternatives were open to David Blakesly?

3   What points are likely to be taken into account by anyone (such as the ACAS conciliation officer, or the Tribunal members) when judging the fairness of the dismissal?

4   What do you think will be the outcome of the case, and why?

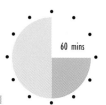

3 Work-based assignment

The time guide for this assignment gives you an approximate idea of how long it is likely to take you to write up your findings. You will find you need to spend some additional time gathering information, talking to colleagues, and thinking about the assignment.

S/NVQ C15.2

Your written response to this assignment may provide the basis of appropriate evidence for your S/NVQ portfolio. The assignment is also designed to help you to demonstrate the following Personal Competences:

- thinking and taking decisions;
- building teams;
- focusing on results.

What you have to do

Look at the key performance indicators for the employee relationship factors within your own team, which might include:

- staff turnover rate – overall;
- staff who leave within three months of appointment;
- sickness absence rate;
- timekeeping;
- participation by team members in union activities, health and safety committees or other voluntary duties;
- disciplinary actions on record;
- team briefings held;
- grievances raised through the grievance procedure;
- use made of reporting systems, such as hazard or near miss schemes and suggestion schemes;
- feedback from appraisal schemes;
- any other factors you believe relevant.

Analyse the data you have available – in confidence – and the trends that you can assess over a period of six months or longer.

Write a report to describe:

1   the particular strengths emerging, on which you can build;

2   the adverse trends which emerge and which need to be reversed;

3   the matters you can only influence with the help of other managers (for example, the quality of recruits or the lack of action taken on reasonable suggestions you have made).

If, for any valid reason, it is impossible for you to access the relevant data for your own team, then use the data presented below for the housekeeping department (employing 12 staff) of a medium-sized seaside hotel for the first three quarters of a year.

The Welcome Guest Hotel
Housekeeping Department

	Reporting period (quarters)		
Key Performance Indicator	Spring	Summer	Autumn
Sickness turnover rate: ■ overall – numbers left/replaced ■ within 3 months of appointment	4 0	10 3	6 1
Sickness absence rate (days/employee/month)	2.6	5.8	2.7
Timekeeping (number of lateness occasions)	4	8	6
Disciplinary actions recorded	1	4	0
Team briefings held	2	0	0
Grievances raised through procedure	0	2	0
Accidents reported	3	11	2

Number of reports made:
   Near miss reports
   Suggestions scheme
	0
	0
		1
		2
			0
			1

Participation by team members
(number of employees involved):
   Union activities
   health and safety committees
   other voluntary duties
	0
	0
	0
		0
		0
		0
			0
			0
			0

Reflect and review

1 Reflect and review

Now that you have completed your work on *Managing Lawfully – People and Employment*, let us review each of our workbook objectives.

The first objective was:

■ When you have worked through this workbook you will be better equipped to comprehend and implement your organization's employment policies and procedures as a major step towards managing your team fairly and consistently within the law.

Employment procedures and policies translate the principles and the developing practice of the law into day-to-day rules and procedures which all managers must implement.

The law itself is evolving continuously and managers rely on senior and specialist managers in their organisations to keep their procedures up to date with essential changes, taking advice from external sources such as ACAS.

■ Are you confident that you know your own organization's procedures sufficiently thoroughly?

_____

■ In practice, do you follow the procedures implicitly, or are there barriers which you need to surmount, personally or with help from your own manager?

_____

_____

The second objective was:

- Manage your team to achieve positive relationships both with you and within the team, recognizing and defusing conflict in the first instance wherever practicable.

First line managers work at the interface between management policies and procedures and employees. They are in the best position to influence employees and create harmonious working relationships by managing their team with respect, applying well established approaches to motivation and communications, and comparing the results obtained with agreed standards of performance.

- Do you believe that you have sufficient knowledge of the approaches you should be using?

- Do you make effective use of them, or are there areas in which you should be doing more and, if so, what additional actions do you plan to take?

The third objective was:

- Deal with disciplinary matters in a fair and consistent way within the law.

Taking formal disciplinary action is a sensitive and difficult process to instigate, especially when it involves people with whom you work every day and on whom you rely to give you support.

It often requires a great deal of moral fibre to act when it would be easy to look the other way – especially where employees have developed their own ways of doing things, which, though against the rules, have become established custom and practice.

Nevertheless, if some employees are allowed to get away with poor standards of performance or conduct, morale will suffer among their peers, or general standards will decline. The disciplinary procedures described, based on ACAS guidance and accepted as fair by the law and by independent trades unions, are there to provide an impersonal, consistent way to bring those who can't, or won't for the time being, meet the standards required back into line with them.

- Are you confident that you know your own organization's procedures sufficiently well and are prepared to apply them without fear or favour?

■ Are there aspects of the procedures you know insufficiently well, or lack confidence to enact? If so, what plans do you have to address the issues?

2 Action plan

Use this plan to develop further for yourself a course of action you want to take. Make a note in the left-hand column of the issues or problems you want to tackle, and then decide what you intend to do, and make a note in column 2.

The resources you need might include time, materials, information or money. You may need to negotiate for some of them, but they could be something easily acquired, like half an hour of somebody's time, or a chapter of a book. Put whatever you need in column 3. No plan means anything without a timescale, so put a realistic target completion date in column 4.

Finally, describe the outcome you want to achieve as a result of this plan, whether it is for your own benefit or advancement, or a more efficient way of doing things.

Desired outcomes

1 Issues	2 Action	3 Resources	4 Target completion

Actual outcomes

3 Extensions

Extension 1	Booklet	Contracts of employment
	Edition	February 2002
	Publisher	ACAS

Extension 2	Booklet	Varying a contract of employment
	Edition	July 2000
	Publisher	ACAS

Extension 3   ACAS produces various leaflets to help you manage effectively within the law.

You can get more information by visiting www.acas.org.uk

Extension 4   You can download booklets, fact sheets and leaflets providing practical guidance on employment relations, regulations and procedures from www.dti.gov.uk/er

Extension 5	Book	Bullying and Harassment at Work – Managers/Employers
	Edition	November 1999
	Publisher	ACAS

Extension 6	Book	Disciplinary and Grievance Procedures
	Edition	September 2000
	Publisher	ACAS

Extension 7	Book	Producing Disciplinary and Grievance Procedures
	Edition	November 2001
	Publisher	ACAS

Extension 8	Book	Producing a Written Statement
	Edition	November 2001
	Publisher	ACAS

Extension 9	Book	Representation at Work
	Edition	January 2002
	Publisher	ACAS

4 Answers to self-assessment questions

Self-assessment 1 on pages 12–13

1   The law impinges on many aspects of employing people, including contracts of employment, equal opportunities, data protection, trade unions, and health, safety and welfare at work.

2   Three ways in which an employer can ensure that its employment policies are communicated effectively to all employees are: providing an employee handbook; providing induction training; and giving regular briefings.

3   **Unfair dismissal, discrimination in regard to race, sex or disability** and **victimization** are three of the main grounds on which an employee can make an application to an Employment Tribunal.

4   Well established grievance procedures help an organization to manage legally by giving employees the chance to raise issues which concern them in a formal way, with built-in safeguards and appeals to independent managers.

5   The main stages in a formal disciplinary procedure as recommended by ACAS are:

    1   recorded verbal warning;
    2   first written warning;
    3   final written warning;
    4   dismissal.

6   An important principle of sound disciplinary procedures is that **no manager** is allowed to dismiss their **immediate** subordinate without reference to a higher level of management.

7   No matter how good a disciplinary procedure is, it will not be effective legally unless it is applied **fairly** and **consistently**.

8   Written records of disciplinary procedures used concerning an individual employee are essential to prove to an **Employment Tribunal** that an organization has acted fairly.

9   Appeal procedures are an essential part of **disciplinary** procedures if they are to be seen as fair by an **Employment Tribunal**.

10 The membership of an employment tribunal comprises a '**chair**' who is legally qualified, a second member with **commercial experience** and a third who has a **practical trade union** background.

**Self-assessment 2
on pages 34–35**

1 Actions that a team leader can take to help earn the respect and trust of the team include:

- knowing the job;
- listening to what team members think;
- setting an example, such as good timekeeping and attendance;
- being available to talk to individuals;
- sticking to what you say;
- tackling individuals' poor performance;
- encouraging people who show promise;
- helping people who have particular temporary problems and needs;
- walking the job at least once each day or shift;
- treating everyone with respect and courtesy.

2 The use of team briefing will ensure that everyone in the team knows **what** is required of them and that everyone gets the **same** message.

3 Team leaders need to be good **listeners** and able to **act** on what they hear when necessary.

4 Team leaders should ensure that all new team members go through an **induction** process when they first join the organization.

5 Assigning **blame** to one party or another is always **unhelpful** in resolving conflict situations.

6 Examples of an individual employee's concerns which a well founded grievance procedure might help resolve include:

- harassment or bullying;
- being passed over for promotion;
- working rotas, holiday arrangements.

7 Custom and practice may be evidence of sub-cultures which, if not addressed, can **undermine** your authority as a leader.

8 Potential benefits to appraisers from using a formal appraisal system are the chance to discuss issues in greater depth and to receive feedback from the 'appraisee' on performance as a team leader.

Potential benefits for the person being appraised are objective feedback on performance and the opportunity to raise issues and concerns in private situation.

Self-assessment 3
on page 76

1   All disciplinary offences involve a **breach of the rules**.

2   If a disciplinary offence is minor, a first line manager might decide that, rather than beginning the formal disciplinary procedure, they should have an **informal discussion** with the team member.

3   **Everybody involved** benefits from there being clear rules for dealing with disciplinary offences.

4   Here are the actions you might take, set out in order.

    e   Decide who should be present.
    b   Decide where the meeting is to be held.
    f   Introduce the participants, and state why they are there.
    i   Give the employee a chance to state his or her case.
    a   Decide what penalty should be imposed.
    h   Sum up what's been said.
    d   Continue to monitor performance.

5   Answers to Activities

Activity 8
on page 17

1   If someone isn't competent to do the job, this is probably because of poor SELECTION and TRAINING.

2   An uncommitted employee often has not had the organization's policies EXPLAINED to them intelligibly.

3   Rivalries between individuals may arise when a team leader apparently FAVOURS some team members by comparison with others.

4   A team leader must EARN the respect of all team members.

Activity 24
on page 51

If you glance back through the procedure, you will see that the correct answers are:

1   Would every minor offence have to be taken through the procedure above? No: as is stated at the start, minor faults are dealt with informally.

2   In which stages do the warnings given become spent or are disregarded after a certain period of time? Stages 1, 2 and 3.

3   After which stages does the employee have a right of appeal? **All** stages.

4   At which stages are the warnings written down? **All** stages.

5   At which stages does the employee receive a written document? Stages 2, 3 and 4.

Activity 27
on page 54

1   **Mrs Jones in the wages department**

It might be difficult convincing someone that this was a disciplinary offence. Some of the reasons are that:

■   her office first line manager knew what was going on;
■   she took as little time as possible – using some of her coffee break;
■   other people had done the same thing, so there was a precedent;
■   her personal circumstances provided a good reason why she wanted to make the collection;
■   she made sure her work was done.

2   **Mrs Jones in the reception area**

You may agree that her behaviour warrants some form of disciplinary action. Some of the reasons you may have put down are that:

■   there is no evidence that she asked anyone's permission;
■   she spent a long time on the collection;
■   she had already been warned about her behaviour;
■   the collection could almost be considered as being for her own benefit;
■   it is part of her job to be in a specific place. In this case, it is important that somebody is there to meet visitors at reception.

If you agreed with my arguments, perhaps you will also agree that these two cases contrasted dramatically. One was clearly not an offence, while the other clearly was. If you have had experience of dealing with disciplinary matters, you will know that decisions are often much more difficult than this.

Activity 32
on page 68

The only answer to this question is: the procedure of the organization where you work.

If there is no agreed procedure, you could follow the example procedure given by ACAS as outlined in Session C. Obviously, any previous offences still on record involving the **same individual** may well affect your decision. Don't forget also that any previous cases involving **different** individuals but the **same offence** should be taken into account: the aim is consistency.

Activity 34
on pages 70–71

You may have noticed a number of ways in which this ending of the interview is an improvement on our last example. The first line manager:

■   stated what the offence was;
■   gave Ray a chance to comment;

- gave the trade union representative the chance to comment;
- told Ray about the company's disciplinary procedure, and what a further offence might lead to;
- told Ray about his right of appeal;
- told Ray that the offence could be erased from the records after six months;
- made clear, unambiguous statements.

6 Answers to the quick quiz

Answer 1   Two of the most important documents employees should normally expect to have to conform with the employment laws are the contract of employment and a written statement of terms and conditions of employment.

Answer 2   Some of the steps which the law may expect an employer to take are: providing proper induction training, helping employees whose first language is not English, and explaining intelligibly the meaning of expressions such as 'gross misconduct'.

Answer 3   Apart from gross misconduct, three ways in which employees might break their contract of employment are: by failing to meet reasonable performance targets, by being late for work, and by failing to observe the procedure for reporting in when absent through sickness.

Answer 4   Employees who believe that they have been dismissed unfairly can apply to an Employment Tribunal to have their case against the former employer heard.

Answer 5   A recognized trade union will be able to represent a member's interests during disciplinary hearings and appeals procedures.

Answer 6   The existence of an appeals procedure in grievance procedures ensures that the employee can take their concerns to a manager who will be reasonably detached from the employee's immediate situation, and whose personal prejudices cannot cloud the issue.

Answer 7   The letters 'ACAS' are an abbreviation for the Advisory, Conciliation and Arbitration Service.

Answer 8   'Custom and practice' is a general term which covers unofficial working methods that have built up over time and that may be at odds with the organization's official policies. If deep rooted, such working methods can make it hard for a manager to apply the proper procedures, even if the law requires it.

Answer 9   Assigning blame to one party or another will tend to make everyone wary of the process and reluctant to get involved in it.

Answer 10   A 'win–win' situation is an outcome from a dispute such that all the parties feel that they have achieved something positive from the process, even if they didn't get *everything* they hoped for. Circumstances where this is not an achievable outcome would include any where to concede something to a party would break the law; for instance, by condoning unsafe practices, or allowing an employee to refuse to work with someone because they were of another race, sex or religion.

Answer 11   Maintaining accurate, up-to-date records is important because:

- legal proceedings may start some time after the events referred to;
- people's memories are unreliable;
- people don't always tell the truth;
- the records will provide concrete evidence that procedures were followed to the letter.

Answer 12   Discipline at work has the four main objectives of: safety; prosperity of the organization; fairness; compliance with a contract.

Answer 13   You should have mentioned: new employees; people who don't speak English as their first language; young people.

Answer 14   Stage 1: oral warning. Stage 2 – Written warning. Stage 3 – Final written warning or disciplinary suspension. Stage 4 – Dismissal.

Answer 15   ACAS suggest that gross misconduct includes: theft, fraud or deliberate falsification of records; fighting, or assault on another person; deliberate damage to company property; serious incapability through alcohol or being under the influence of illegal drugs; serious negligence which causes unacceptable loss, damage or injury; serious acts of insubordination.

Answer 16   We said that the purposes of a disciplinary interview are to:

- allow the employee to give his or her version of the incident;
- ensure a full discussion, so that everyone present has a chance to hear the facts and to present any new facts;
- advise the employee of his or her rights;
- enable a fair judgement to be made so that an appropriate penalty can be awarded.

7 Certificate

Completion of this certificate by an authorized person shows that you have worked through all the parts of this workbook and satisfactorily completed the assessments. The certificate provides a record of what you have done that may be used for exemptions or as evidence of prior learning against other nationally certificated qualifications.

Pergamon Flexible Learning and ILM are always keen to refine and improve their products. One of the key sources of information to help this process are people who have just used the product. If you have any information or views, good or bad, please pass these on.

INSTITUTE OF LEADERSHIP & MANAGEMENT

SUPERSERIES

Managing Lawfully –
People and Employment

....

has satisfactorily completed this workbook

Name of signatory ....

Position ....

Signature ....

Date ....

Official stamp

Fourth Edition

INSTITUTE OF LEADERSHIP & MANAGEMENT
SUPERSERIES
FOURTH EDITION

Achieving Quality	0 7506 5874 6
Appraising Performance	0 7506 5838 X
Becoming More Effective	0 7506 5887 8
Budgeting for Better Performance	0 7506 5880 0
Caring for the Customer	0 7506 5840 1
Collecting Information	0 7506 5888 6
Commitment to Equality	0 7506 5893 2
Controlling Costs	0 7506 5842 8
Controlling Physical Resources	0 7506 5886 X
Delegating Effectively	0 7506 5816 9
Delivering Training	0 7506 5870 3
Effective Meetings at Work	0 7506 5882 7
Improving Efficiency	0 7506 5871 1
Information in Management	0 7506 5890 8
Leading Your Team	0 7506 5839 8
Making a Financial Case	0 7506 5892 4
Making Communication Work	0 7506 5875 4
Managing Change	0 7506 5879 7
Managing Lawfully – Health, Safety and Environment	0 7506 5841 X
Managing Lawfully – People and Employment	0 7506 5853 3
Managing Relationships at Work	0 7506 5891 6
Managing Time	0 7506 5877 0
Managing Tough Times	0 7506 5817 7
Marketing and Selling	0 7506 5837 1
Motivating People	0 7506 5836 3
Networking and Sharing Information	0 7506 5885 1
Organizational Culture and Context	0 7506 5884 3
Organizational Environment	0 7506 5889 4
Planning and Controlling Work	0 7506 5813 4
Planning Training and Development	0 7506 5860 6
Preventing Accidents	0 7506 5835 5
Project and Report Writing	0 7506 5876 2
Securing the Right People	0 7506 5822 3
Solving Problems	0 7506 5818 5
Storing and Retrieving Information	0 7506 5894 0
Understanding Change	0 7506 5878 9
Understanding Finance	0 7506 5815 0
Understanding Quality	0 7506 5881 9
Working In Teams	0 7506 5814 2
Writing Effectively	0 7506 5883 5

To order – phone us direct for prices and availability details
(please quote ISBNs when ordering) on 01865 888190